BREATHE *mama* BREATHE

BREATHE mama BREATHE

5-Minute Mindfulness for Busy Moms

Shonda Moralis, MSW, LCSW

Cover and text design by Sarah Smith
Author photograph by Elaine Zelker

First published in India in 2019 by agreement with The Experiment.

ISBN 978-81-8328-542-1

Published by
Wisdom Tree
4779/23, Ansari Road
Darya Ganj, New Delhi-110 002
Ph.: 011-23247966/67/68
wisdomtreebooks@gmail.com

Printed in India

To my parents, Linda and Richard Bear

And to Erik, Anika, and Ben

With immeasurable love and gratitude

In giving birth to our babies, we may find that
we give birth to new possibilities within ourselves.

—Myla and Jon Kabat-Zinn

CONTENTS

CHAPTER 3

Connecting with Your Family During the Day . . . 71

CHAPTER 4

Connecting with Yourself During the Day . . . 141

INTRODUCTION

The Breathe, Mama, Breathe Plan

Mindfulness for Mom in Five Minutes a Day

"How are you?"

"Good . . . busy. Really busy!"

Sound familiar? *Busy* is the standard mom reply. Our kids are highly enriched; our homes are clean(ish); we've taken on yet another commitment and are valiantly attempting to keep it all together. What I want to know is this: How are you *really*?

Fulfilled? Content? At ease? If you dig down for an honest answer, your eyes may fill with tears as you admit to an emotional, overwhelmed no. Honest answers may sound more like this:

- I am stressed out, exhausted, and have no time for myself.
- The balance is off in my life. The pace feels too frantic and out of control.
- I yell at my children more than I enjoy them.
- Even when I am spending time with my kids, I am often distractedly running through my to-do list or checking my phone once again.
- I feel guilty that I am not doing enough. How do all those other moms manage to balance it all?

I've found that with just five minutes a day of consistent mindfulness meditation practice, however, my day is much different:

- I remain more calm and aware throughout the day.

- I am more in control of my responses to stressful situations rather than reacting habitually and in less-than-ideal ways.
- I look forward to those five minutes of quiet, rest, and calm and miss them when a day passes without them.
- I feel more connected with my children, partner, and the simple things in life.
- I have learned to automatically drop my tense shoulders and take a few full breaths throughout the day.
- I smile more, laugh more, and play more.

The term *mindfulness* seems to be omnipresent these days. Just google it and you can spend hours lost in practically infinite sources of information about it and its applications. Everyone's doing it: Oprah, the Seattle Seahawks, Congressman Tim Ryan, and companies such as Google, Apple, and IBM. *Time* magazine even had a cover story entitled "The Mindful Revolution." But what exactly *is* mindfulness?

Have you ever gotten into your car and arrived at a destination with little recollection of actually driving there? Most of us have. This is an example of our minds operating on autopilot, and many busy moms often move through life this way—distracted, only partially aware, and with a chronic sense of missing the moment.

Mindfulness, essentially the opposite of autopilot, is the practice of deliberately bringing our attention to the present moment with kindness. It's a way of being in and perceiving the world. Rather than ruminating about the past (either recent or long ago) or imagining the future (worrying or what-ifing), mindfulness encourages us to be present for our lives. It helps us cope with the difficulties while more readily savoring the good times.

The benefits of mindfulness are hard to deny. Shown to increase attention, optimism, and an overall sense of well-being while decreasing anxiety and depression, regular mindfulness practice literally changes the structure and function of the brain. In a study done by Britta Holzel and colleagues using magnetic resonance images (MRI) of the brain, participants who had meditated daily for eight weeks showed an increase in gray matter in the brain (the part of the brain responsible for learning, memory, self-awareness, compassion, and introspection) and a decrease in the size of the amygdala (the area responsible for anxiety and stress). The study concluded that with daily meditation practice, we can remarkably alter our brains for the better, enabling us to think and plan more clearly while reacting with less anxiety and stress. Just as when we exercise and lift weights and the muscles in our bodies are visibly built and strengthened, we can meditate to increase the size and strength of skillful parts of our brains. We have long recognized the benefits of regular physical exercise for our overall well-being, and now we're finding similar benefits with meditation as exercise for our brains. And you don't need hours upon hours of meditation to benefit. Research by Christopher Moyer and colleagues showed positive changes in the brain after just five cumulative hours of meditation.

A fascinating study led by Barbara Fredrickson found that compassion meditation increases positive emotions (such as contentment, joy, love, pride, gratitude, hope, interest, and awe), which open us to positive experiences (such as increased mindfulness, social support, purpose in life, and decrease in symptoms of illness), which, in turn, transform us emotionally and physically for the better—increasing overall life satisfaction and decreasing depressive symptoms. Her research also shows that a more positive outlook on life is one we can choose and cultivate because only 50 percent of our genes determine our happiness. Of the other 50 percent, 10 percent is due to circumstance while a *remarkable 40 percent of our happiness is under our control.* Regular compassion meditation allows us to train our brains and our bodies, positively affecting both emotional and physical long-term health.

Not only does regular meditation practice condition us to stress less, enjoy more, and experience an overall increased sense of happiness, it also has been shown to improve our immune system. In a study by Richard J. Davidson, founder of the Center for Healthy Minds at the University of Wisconsin–Madison, research participants were divided into two groups—one group meditated daily for eight weeks; the other group received no meditation training. At the end of the eight weeks, participants from both groups were given an influenza vaccine. Results showed increased antibodies to the vaccines in the meditators, whereas there was no change in antibodies in the non-meditators. Davidson's research indicates that daily mindfulness meditation actually increases immune response, which means we are able to fight all those germs our kids bestow upon us with more vigor and stay healthy more often. As busy moms, we all know sick days are hard, if not impossible, to come by.

There are now hundreds of studies documenting the wide-ranging benefits of mindfulness meditation. However, much of the mindfulness research is based on an average of twenty to thirty minutes of daily meditation—a wonderful, albeit unrealistic, expectation for most busy mamas. What I have come to realize is that if we believe we must carve out a minimum of twenty to thirty minutes a day, we often don't do it. Good intentions become just that and with no follow through. Simply put, if you don't make the time for mindfulness, you won't see the benefits.

I know from experience. As a devoted mindfulness meditator and teacher, psychotherapist, and experienced mom, I was caught unaware when the birth of my second child a decade after the first left me feeling slightly unhinged. As a second-time mom, I had no delusions about the impending intensity of adding a newborn to our family. After the first few harrowing weeks with a newborn and after the haze of brutal sleep deprivation subsided, it became clear that a daily thirty minutes was not in my near future. Opposed to throwing the baby out with the mindfulness bathwater, I needed to find a way to stay connected to mindfulness and meditation in a more flexible, manageable way.

As the months ticked by, my daily meditation time increased slowly and incrementally, with many stops and starts along the way. What really sustained me through this time, though, was unearthing small ways to infuse my life with mindfulness. It was not only a lifeline when things felt overwhelming, but also a means of savoring the beautiful moments that arose within even the most monotonous of days with a newborn.

Although the jury is still out regarding the ideal length of time to meditate, after more than a decade of teaching mindfulness, what I have repeatedly observed is that five minutes a day of meditation is enough to reap clear and convincing benefits. Research by Elisha Goldstein has shown significant positive emotional effects (such as a greater sense of connection, gratitude, and peace) on well-being and stress with just five minutes a day of mindfulness.

Breathe, Mama, Breathe is my answer to an ongoing search of how to, as best I can, stay true to my deepest held values while juggling my many roles along the way. Working from my years as a therapist and my own life experiences, I've drawn on the science and research of Positive Psychology (the science of happiness and well-being) and mindfulness to offer simple five-minute mindfulness practices specifically designed with busy moms in mind.

We have all our answers inside if we simply allow ourselves a bit of time to get quiet, listen, and reconnect to ourselves. My aim is to teach busy moms simple ways to live more mindfully and with increased energy and peace. When you are feeling balanced, your family reaps the benefits of a mom who is thriving and modeling how to live with more presence, gratitude, and joy. We need to ask ourselves what more we could genuinely wish for our children, our families, and ourselves.

What's the Difference Between Mindfulness and Meditation?

Mindfulness is paying attention to the present moment with purpose and without judgment. Jon Kabat-Zinn beautifully describes it not just as mere presence and attention, but as "presence of heart." It can also be considered simply as a form of exercise used to strengthen your brain.

Mindfulness meditation is just one type of meditation among many, such as transcendental meditation and yoga. Learning to meditate daily is the framework that lays the foundation for a life filled with more mindful awareness. Although meditation is a fairly straightforward practice, it's not always easy, and it's therefore helpful to have some guidance along your mindfulness journey. Much like learning to swim or play the piano, merely reading the instructions isn't enough to acquire the skill. It takes a bit of discipline and effort to learn a stroke in the water or play a song. Likewise, you must actually sit down and meditate for those five minutes each day to reap the powerful benefits.

Ideally, when we meditate we are cultivating a healthy balance of alertness and relaxation as we become increasingly familiar with the busy workings of our mind. The more relaxed and alert we are, the more we're able to live with awareness and clarity. Some use the analogy of a snow globe. When we are very young and our basic needs are met, there are few stressors and life feels calm. Our minds are clear, much like the snow globe at rest.

As we grow and our responsibilities increase, the snow that had been calmly settled on the bottom begins to be shaken. More stress, more shaking, and soon we are unable to see clearly through the snow. Our thoughts and minds are clouded and murky. If we simply pause, take a few breaths, and stop shaking the globe, the snow begins to settle, much like our thoughts. The stressors are still there, just like the snow in the globe, but we are now able to see a bit more clearly and calmly. This is the power of mindfulness meditation.

Mindfulness is pulling ourselves out of autopilot and being aware of what is happening right now and at any time throughout the day. Meditation is the time set aside to practice in some formal way, either in a seated meditation (such as awareness of the breath), in mindful movement (yoga or walking), or a body scan (practiced lying down).

The Power of Shared Success Stories

All too often, the media presents us images of perfect mothering. This is simply not reality. Mothering is messy and wonderful, maddening and blissful, and one of the most paradoxical relationships we will ever enter into. Most of us don't talk about it, though. Many of us hold our insecurities, doubts, and unskillful parenting moments hidden, allowing the embarrassment to grow into shame and secrecy. It's tough to talk about our mistakes and our less-than-perfect moments, but it's so liberating.

When we are honest and authentic in our conversations with other moms, we invite them to speak openly about their struggles, thereby offering one another support and empathy. We are more free to champion one another rather than compare and judge. The more accurately we view the façade of perfect motherhood, the less pressure we put on ourselves to achieve what is obtainable only at great cost to ourselves and our families.

I distinctly remember a few short conversations with other moms that helped pull me through some trying moments with my newborn daughter as she cried incessantly for hours, suffering with acid reflux. One was a passing comment my sister-in-law made about a moment she had with her son as an infant. She told me how, during a particularly tough day, she retreated to her garage and sat weeping, convinced she could not handle this mothering thing. The other was with a long-time friend whose son also had acid reflux as an infant; she was a great support simply by commiserating with me during a fifteen-minute phone call.

In my most trying moments I clung to their words, soothed just hearing that I wasn't alone. I later mentioned to the same friend how much that conversation had meant to me and was surprised to hear she had no recollection of it. To her, she was merely offering comfort in a stressful moment; to me it was a lifeline. We should never underestimate the power of well-placed empathy, honesty, and connection. Along with learning to take mindful breaks, I hope you find self-compassion, comfort, and inspiration in the anecdotes and success stories I share as we travel together through this amazing, life-changing journey called motherhood.

I am, however, cautious with the word *success*. Success, in this case, does not equal perfection, nor does it mean that I or the moms featured throughout *Breathe, Mama, Breathe* have reached some permanent state of mothering nirvana. No, this is real life with real challenges with real children. What I mean by success is that these mindful mamas have found a way to seamlessly and imperfectly weave mindfulness into their full lives despite the unpredictability and tribulations motherhood consistently throws our way. Although each of our situations is unique, there are common threads that show up repeatedly. As you identify with some of their struggles, I believe you will also find courage, hope, and useful suggestions. Be bold, be curious, and be adventurous. All you need to do is get started. I wholeheartedly invite you to join us and become your own *Breathe, Mama, Breathe* success story.

The first part of *Breathe, Mama, Breathe* shows you how to incorporate five-minute daily meditation into your day. Your meditation practice will provide a foundation of balance and ease in your life. By carving out just five minutes each day, you can establish a habit of mindfulness that is proven to decrease stress and increase your overall well-being.

After you learn the basics of mindfulness and have created a daily meditation practice, you may still need extra help when the chaos is at a fever pitch. As we know all too well, those stressful moments can happen morning, noon, or (the middle of the) night, which is where the mindful breaks come in. Mindful breaks are life-lines, life enhancers, reminders, and guides designed to fit seamlessly into the midst of your day. Used to infuse your life with more calm and energy, mindful breaks offer a multitude of ways to step off the treadmill of busyness and bring yourself back to the present moment.

Keep *Breathe, Mama, Breathe* on your bedside table and refer to it when you need some inspiration, a quick mindful break, a laugh, or a lifeline. Highlight, take notes, mark up your copy. Make it a living, breathing, adjustable guide to support your journey through mindful motherhood. Take your commitment to your daily meditation practice seriously; it is serious in that it can change so much in your life for the better. But don't forget to have fun with it. And may you remember, above all else, to breathe, Mama, breathe.

Setting Up Your Daily Five-Minute Meditation

Mindfulness meditation builds increased awareness, calm, and an overall sense of well-being. Sri K. Pattabhi Jois, who brought Ashtanga yoga to the West, said that yoga is 99 percent practice and 1 percent theory. The same holds true for meditation. It's vital that you prioritize and protect your five minutes of meditation practice every day.

When: Choose a time of day and make it a habit. Habits are most easily formed if we bookend them with other already-established habits; for example, waking in the morning, washing your face, sitting to meditate, and then enjoying your daily cup of tea or coffee. Experiment with the best time of day for you. I have found that early morning is the best time for me, before everyone in the house begins stirring. I also love how it sets the tone for my day. Others find that the kids' nap time or bedtime is their best bet. As long as you can stay awake, what is most important is that it becomes part of your daily routine.

Where: As best you can, find a quiet place where you will not be interrupted. Set firm boundaries with yourself and your family that this is *your* time and should be interrupted only in case of emergency. When I've needed to practice in the middle of the day, I have, on occasion, resorted to sitting in my closet for a bit more peace. Of course, we cannot control all variables; the neighbor's dog will bark, the phone will ring. Simply allow these sounds to become a part of your meditation.

Why (am I doing this again?): There will certainly come a time when you ask yourself why you are taking these precious five minutes to sit and do nothing. Remind yourself that you are taking this time to nurture a healthy brain, much like eating a nutritious breakfast sustains your energy and builds a healthy body. Just as you wouldn't leave the house in the morning without eating (or shouldn't), try not to leave without some mindfulness practice as well. Over time, you will miss it when you don't practice and will look forward to this time to nurture yourself. You are worth the time, and your family will benefit as well.

How: It's often helpful, but not necessary, to begin meditating with a guided audio recording. Like learning any new skill, when you practice regularly it will become more familiar and comfortable. After some time you may realize you are just as comfortable practicing on your own. You can learn to meditate with either the instructions that follow or by visiting my Web site—shondamoralis.net—where you will find various free guided meditations along with links to many other meditation resources.

1. Find a chair in which your feet comfortably touch the ground, or sit on the floor on pillows so your bottom and hips are raised off the floor. Sit up tall, straighten the spine, relax the shoulders, and allow the eyes to close.

2. Pause and become aware of sensations in your body with a sense of curiosity and acceptance. You can do this by slowly scanning through your body, starting with your feet and systematically moving up to your head. Do you notice tightness anywhere? Are your shoulders raised toward your ears? Is your brow furrowed? Can you soften those areas?

3. Now relax your belly, noticing it rise and fall as the breath naturally comes and goes. When your mind wanders (which happens to everyone), notice where your mind was (planning, remembering, judging) and simply return your attention—with kindness for yourself—to the breath and begin again. It may be helpful to silently note *rising* and *falling* as you notice the breath come and go. See if you can notice the beginning and

ending of the inhale, the beginning and ending of the exhale, and perhaps a pause happening naturally in between. Each time your mind wanders, gently bring it back to the sensations of breathing in the belly. If you need to bring your attention back fifty times as you sit for five minutes, that is perfectly fine.

4. Congratulate yourself for carving out time, sitting, and staying. It's important we cultivate this attitude of awareness outside of our meditation practice time as well. Really, what good is your meditation if you leave your five minutes of stillness and commence frantically dashing through the next part of your day?

5. Proceed with your day and any combination of mindful breaks.

Bring an attitude of curiosity and playfulness to your meditation time. Let go of expectations and goals and simply observe what arises. Just as with parenting, consistency and flexibility are essential to meditation. Oh, yes, and don't forget your sense of humor. The thoughts that arise during meditation can be quite amusing. Accept each practice as it is, but try not to lose sight of the effortlessness of mindfulness. The goal itself is not relaxation, although it is often a welcome side effect.

> Blessed are they who laugh at themselves, for they will never cease to be amused.
>
> —*Anonymous*

As best you can, practice every day. On pages 262–63 you'll find a Mindfulog, a space to record your mindful breaks, which you may find helpful in tracking your daily practice and keeping you accountable. You can create a new copy for each week (download blank copies from shondamoralis.net). In the 5-Minute Meditation blocks, you may want to write the time of day you meditated and what you noticed. For example, *felt restless and distracted* or *felt calm and relaxed.* In the Mindful Break blocks you can either identify one to three different mindful breaks that you will practice over the course of the week or change them up each day. Here, too, record what you notice as you incorporate more mindfulness into your day. For example, for Homework Mindful Break, *Calmed myself before diving into homework with Maddie. She stayed calm. No argument!*

There will come a time, however, when life happens—let's say the stomach flu relentlessly makes its way through your family—and you miss a day (or two or three) of meditation practice. Don't waste time or energy judging yourself. Fortunately, with mindfulness, each moment is an opportunity to start anew. Simply get right back on track and begin again today.

Including Partners

When I mention *Breathe, Mama, Breathe* to papas, they often reply, "Hey, what about us dads? We get stressed out, too." Yes, of course, and I am all for mindful, meditating fathers. I love teaching mindful parenting courses when both parents show up and are ready to learn. A double dose of mindfulness for our kids and a partner doing his own mindful work? That is seriously awesome.

Although fathers have certainly come far in the past few decades regarding shared parenting responsibilities, I wrote *Breathe, Mama, Breathe* specifically for busy moms because, even if our partners have split the responsibilities quite evenly, there continue to be societal pressures and expectations specific only to moms. Those expectations of having it all are still going strong. We still have a ways to go. And bottom line, "If Mama ain't happy, ain't nobody happy."

So by all means, let your partner in on your own *Breathe, Mama, Breathe* plan. You may want to explain the importance of your five quiet minutes alone and may need to enlist his support in making it happen. Before long he will notice the difference in you and may freely encourage you to take the time.

Invite him to meditate. Involve him in the many mindful breaks. Share your copy of *Breathe, Mama, Breathe* with him. If your partner is not a dad but also a mom, buy her a copy. If you are a single mom, you may want to share *Breathe, Mama, Breathe* with your children's caregivers so they can benefit from and model mindfulness in their own lives and while caring for your kids. Two mindful parents or caregivers are greater than the sum of their parts.

Not everyone's partner will want to meditate, though, and that's perfectly fine. Take mine, for example. Occasionally, some people allude to the imaginary assumption that if they showed up at my house at any given time, not only would the entire household ooze Zen, but they might catch us all sitting on the floor in a circle, cross-legged, chanting Om. Om, yeah— no. In fact, my husband does not meditate, although I would contend that as a musician and a poet, he is naturally quite mindful in his awareness. Of course, when I began meditating more than ten years ago I encouraged him to try it. Hoping he'd succumb to a little positive peer pressure, I shared how a handful of his favorite musicians, such as Eddie Vedder and Ben Harper, were reported faithful meditators. Alas, he did not capitulate and, eventually, I let it go. He may one day decide to give it a try, but for now, for our family, it works. Your partner definitely does not need to practice mindfulness for your family to reap the far-reaching benefits of your practice. Take care of yourself, and they will soon benefit from the inevitable trickle-down effect.

Family Practices

When someone asks me at what age children can begin meditating, I share a story of my then eight-month-old son. It was bedtime, I was exhausted, and I was having an overwhelmed "Calgon, take-me-away!" moment. Holding my little guy in my arms in a gentle bear hug, I began taking a few long, deep breaths to calm myself. To my amazement he slowly began lengthening his breaths, synchronizing them with mine. Right before my eyes he was learning to become aware of, bring his attention to, and control his breathing—at eight months old. No, he was not formally meditating, silently noting his inhale and exhale, but he was clearly forming the basis of breath awareness. Obviously too young to understand verbal instructions, my little guy was learning by unintentional mindful example. And although he is many awesome things, he is not a little mindfulness child prodigy. Every child has an innate capacity for mindfulness and meditation. And if you are practicing mindfulness, your children will automatically assimilate it to some degree as well. The short answer to the question, then, is that children of all ages can be taught to meditate, however basic the building blocks.

Both the five-minute meditations and many mindful breaks in this book can be practiced with your children. By all means, I encourage you to teach your children explicitly about meditation and mindfulness whenever possible. There are many ways we can do it. We can teach our kids directly, allow them to see more organically through modeling how mindfulness enhances our lives, or some combination of the two. There are also many wonderful books, CDs, and videos available to support you in this endeavor. Much of it depends on your children's ages and their willingness to try something new. Younger kids are more apt to be curious and want to emulate your practice. If you have teens, they may not want to model much of anything related to you (for the next decade or so). Sure, you can talk about it with them and share simple practices. As best you can, meet them where they are without forcing anything. Whenever possible, lead by example.

If you are disappointed your children show no interest in practicing with you, let it rest for a while. Meditation is something that cannot be coerced; our kids can easily see through our complicated ruses straight to our mindfulness agenda. So let your practice affect them naturally, however it will. If you gently expose them to the variety of ways to practice mindfulness, they will inevitably absorb some. I encourage you to check your own agenda periodically. This practice is for you and not some child-improvement project, even if generated out of love.

If you do meditate with your children, I strongly encourage you to use it as a supplement to your meditation time, making sure you continue to practice on your own as well. It's important to protect those five minutes for yourself because, regardless of how well behaved your children are, as you practice together you will be thinking about them and their meditation experience rather than your own. However much you involve and teach your family, remember to always put on your own oxygen mask first.

When to Take Your Stripped-Down (Yet Incredibly Powerful) Mindful Breaks

I highly encourage you to take time for dedicated mindfulness meditation practice every day. But what about the other moments in your day when you need to reset and refocus? The beauty of mindfulness is that we can take a mindful break anytime, anywhere. Like any practice, the more we remember to bring our attention to the moment, the easier it becomes. We can dramatically enrich the quality of our lives by making small, deliberate adjustments in our behavior. These intentional changes have a ripple effect, allowing us to make space in our lives for what truly matters.

Mindful breaks are strategies for when we find ourselves in challenging moments and need immediate access to some calm. They also highlight the ordinary, beautiful moments we often miss when we are operating on autopilot. The following mindful breaks offer varied ways for you to live your mindfulness practice throughout the day. We begin with the Foundational Mindful Breaks, which teach the fundamentals of mindfulness. Emphasizing the interconnectedness of the mind and body, these mindful breaks can be used as building blocks for your mindfulness practice. Additional chapters are organized within the larger framework of daily life. Some are designed to be used at the beginning of your day or as your day is winding down. Others focus on strategies for self-care, connecting with your family, and handling situations in the larger world. Some breaks are universal and can be used at any time at any stage of parenting. Others were written with specific stages in mind—such as teaching your teen to drive, bottle- or breast-feeding your newborn, or during homework time.

You may want to begin with one new mindful break, progressively adding another new practice every few days. Before you know it, you will have seamlessly added many mindful breaks into your daily repertoire. Feel free to mix and match and even create your own versions to suit your family's unique needs and circumstances. Mindful breaks can help transform the unpleasant into bearable, chaos into calm, and the ordinary into extraordinary.

Here is how a few moms have made mindful breaks work for them:

Sara, a married, well-educated, stay-at-home mom of three little guys under the age of six, taught her boys and husband to use the Three-Breath Hug (page 77) each night after dinner, soon morphing it into their very own giggly Three-Breath Family Group Hug. She practiced the Powerful Pause (page 38) at various points throughout her day, reminding herself to take a breath and slow down just a bit. Instead of these small changes feeling overwhelming and forced, Sara told me she found them to flow easily and seamlessly into the midst of her day. She was amazed at how calm and at ease she felt while still accomplishing what needed to get done.

One seemingly ordinary day, Sara's five-year-old came up to her, wrapped his little arms around her neck, gazed into her eyes, and said, "Mommy, I love when you are happy and smiling. You are so much fun to play with!" Sara, recalling this moment with tears in her eyes, recognized how her mindfulness practice had positively impacted her family life as well.

Nicole, a work-outside-the-home mom of two teens, told me how she began practicing the Waking with Gratitude Mindful Break (page 51) before rising from bed in the morning. She shared her surprise at automatically offering gratitude more easily and often to her husband and kids, soon noticing its infectiousness as her family began to thank her and show more appreciation for all she does (not a small feat for two teenagers). Nicole has now also learned to recognize when she needs to take a few deep breaths, set firm boundaries, or steal away for a five-minute SNAP Break (page 46). Her family encourages it because they have seen the positive changes in her. Nicole told me, "Without exaggeration, mindfulness saved my sanity. I was feeling overwhelmed and unappreciated. Some days are still really hard, but my mindfulness practice reminds me that tomorrow is another day, and I can always count on those few deep breaths to get me through anything."

Carolyn, a single working mom to three children, ages twenty, fifteen, and twelve, also cares for her nearby aging parents. She told me (with a laugh) that now she actually enjoys setting the coffeemaker each evening in anticipation of her morning Coffee Mindful Break (pages 54–55). Feeling pulled in so many directions and especially scattered in the morning, Carolyn also began practicing the Prepping for Tomorrow Mindful Break (page 255) and taught her three children to integrate it into their evening routines as well. Prior to this routine, Carolyn said she would inevitably end up frustrated and yelling at "at least one child who should have known better and planned better—not that I didn't remind them all the time to gather their things—or a child crying or angry." Not only did this mindful break allow for a much more peaceful start to their morning, it inspired her children to be more independent by taking responsibility for remembering what was needed.

In addition to utilizing mindful breaks that suited their respective busy lives, each of these moms made their five-minute meditations a daily priority. Likewise, you will derive the most benefit from partaking in a daily combination of five-minute meditation practice and mindful breaks. Mindfulness practice, for me, has meant more presence, more joy, more laughter, more fun, more connection, more compassion, more balance, and more deliberate choices in the way I spend my days. And this, too, is what I wish for you.

CHAPTER 1

Foundational Mindful Breaks

We all want our kids to be happy, to be at ease so they can enjoy and live up to their greatest potential in life. The very real epidemic of stress and busyness in our society affects us all, though, threatening our prosperity, our health, and our overall sense of well-being. Unfortunately, our children are not immune. As busy moms, we are willing to do whatever necessary to ensure our kids are given the best we can provide, often neglecting our own happiness as a vital component to their success. Internalizing the misguided societal notion that taking time for ourselves is selfish and self-indulgent, we buy into the erroneous message that our kids need us more than we need those few renewing moments to ourselves.

The necessity of putting on our own oxygen masks first, however, is a cliché for a reason. When our air supply (read *energy*) is depleted, we are rather useless to our families. Not to mention, moods are highly contagious; therefore, our anxiety and unhappiness do not go unnoticed. Our kids sense and absorb our moods including our level of stress, whether we try to keep it under wraps or not.

When my children are melting down, I take it as a cue to investigate my reactions and attitudes as a helpful reminder to examine how the contagiousness of my current mood may be contributing to the situation. It's not that I don't hold my kids responsible for their actions or blame myself for their misbehavior. It's that in many cases their behavior is an accurate barometer of my level of stress at the moment. Conversely, have you noticed how on those days when you are calm and rested, your interactions with your kids are also more peaceful? For better or worse, kids soak up our emotions and reactions like little sponges. They feel our anxieties, our worries, our joy, or our sense of ease.

Fortunately, all it takes to resuscitate ourselves (and by extension our families) with increased vitality and calm is to create small pockets of time in our days to breathe. We can deliberately cultivate a sense of calm and ease in our homes with brief moments of mindfulness, thereby softening the effects of stress and busyness. What a gift to our families. What a gift to ourselves. And, regardless of your stage of mothering, each of us can benefit from consistent mindful reminders.

The following breaks provide the foundation to the overall concept of mindfulness. Because they are more general in nature, they can be practiced at any time of day and as often as you feel necessary. As you work through the rest of the mindful breaks, it may help you to refer to them occasionally (particularly the Triangle of Awareness break) if you need a refresher on where your focus should be during your mindful breaks or if you simply need five minutes to reset and refresh.

Triangle of Awareness

The Triangle of Awareness is a helpful framework to conceptualize that mindfulness consists of our body sensations (including the breath), our thoughts, and our emotions. Each of these aspects can be diagrammed as a point on a triangle, with mindful awareness in the center. These three points (body sensations, thoughts, and emotions) mutually impact the other, just as our minds and bodies are very much interconnected. When an intense emotion is triggered, you can be sure there will be some strong body sensations and thoughts accompanying the emotion as well.

To illustrate, consider this example: It's a school day morning and my daughter has yet to get dressed and brush her teeth and hair. I gaze over at the clock and realize that it is now 6:45 AM, and the bus due to arrive in a mere fifteen minutes. My first thought is, *She may not make it to the bus stop on time*. I then notice my heart rate begin to accelerate just a bit (body sensation), triggering the emotions of frustration and anxiety. I now say to my daughter in a slightly high-pitched tone, "You need to speed it up or you will miss the bus!" My next thought is that if she does in fact miss the bus, I will need to drive her twenty minutes out of my way to school, causing me to be late to work and late for my first patient of the day. Cue the tight jaw muscles, raised shoulders, and increased breathing and heart rate (body sensations). You can see how each point on the triangle mutually influences one another in a bit of a domino effect. Here is where our mindfulness practice can be of great benefit if we are aware enough to apply it.

> Between stimulus and response there is a space. In that space is our power to choose our response. In our response lies our growth and our freedom.
>
> *—Victor Frankl*

Depending on my state of mindfulness in that moment, I may react in one of two ways. On a day when I'm not at my best and most aware, I might snap at my daughter, "Hurry *up*! I am tired of rushing out the door in the morning!" No longer aware of my thoughts, feelings, or emotions, and even less aware of my behavior, words, and actions, I have been emotionally hijacked by my stress. This scenario might play out with tears and raised voices and feelings of guilt for losing it unnecessarily (*What kind of mindfulness teacher are you anyway?*).

On a more mindful day I would have the wherewithal to pause, notice my body sensations (*Whoa, my shoulders are practically touching my ears. My jaw is tense.*), take a few breaths, and react in a much more thoughtful way: “Honey, we really need to get moving so we can make it to the bus on time.” The chances of my daughter responding well are much greater, and my blood pressure remains within normal range. I have now responded to the stressful situation rather than merely reacting in an old, habitual, and unhelpful way. When we lose perspective it feels overwhelming and serious, but when we are able to pause and step back, we see the threat was merely our perception and the result of spinning around the triangle.

The Triangle of Awareness Mindful Break: At any point throughout the day, pause and notice what is present on the three points of the triangle, which can be done whether or not a challenging situation has arisen. What body sensations are you experiencing? Perhaps your brow is knit in worry, your shoulders are tense, and your hands clench. What thoughts are present? Is there judging? Imagining? Worry? What about emotions? Is there frustration, hurt, anger, happiness? As best you can, accept what is already here rather than try to deny or change it.

The more you practice this mindful break, the easier it will become to identify sensations, thoughts, and emotions that may not be initially obvious. Simply observing and naming them is often enough to offer us a moment to gather ourselves, take a few deep breaths, and choose a different direction for our reactions. Have patience with yourself as you learn and experiment with the triangle. Forgive yourself when you handle a situation unmindfully, and know that this is the practice of a lifetime. There is always another opportunity right around the corner.

Step Out of Autopilot

Remember all those times when you drove to a routine destination and realized on arrival that you had no recollection of passing familiar landmarks along the way? Even if you were behaving—not texting, not talking on the phone, not eating—you were lost in your thoughts and completely somewhere else in your mind. You may have been planning your shopping list, imagining an upcoming event, or remembering a conversation from the day prior. Author and meditation teacher Tara Brach, PhD, speaks of finding yourself in a virtual reality, which is the antithesis of mindfulness.

What we are training ourselves to do with mindfulness practice is to notice more often when we have been living in that virtual reality, gently bringing ourselves back to the present, and spending more time right here, right now. It is impossible to halt the natural flow of thoughts and mind-wandering. In fact, some daydreaming can be a wonderful thing. Creativity, hopes, and dreams are born out of this. So why is it so important that we train our brains to live more in the present moment? Because when we are living in the present moment rather than in that virtual reality of which Dr. Brach speaks, we have a choice in how we live and how we react. Otherwise, we are really not in control of our responses and choices. We are merely reacting habitually without much awareness or intention.

There are times when being in the moment is seriously unpleasant, instances when we may, consciously or not, avoid being there because it seems too painful or intense. Denial can be temporarily helpful, but when we remain in denial, we establish unhealthy, often addictive patterns of coping. If we are not mindful, we usually find some way to numb ourselves from intense thoughts and feelings. Overeating, drinking alcohol to excess, and illegal drug use are all well-known unhealthy habits some resort to when feeling stressed. There are also, of course, the more culturally approved habits of workaholism and busyness. Because the latter are not only more socially acceptable but also regularly encouraged and revered in our busy culture, it often takes a wake-up call in the form of illness, relationship loss, or other major life crisis before the pervasive negative effects become apparent.

What all these unhealthy patterns have in common is that they serve the sole purpose of helping a person avoid what feels uncomfortable, whether in thoughts, emotions, or body sensations. By intentionally and compassionately bringing our awareness to these habitual coping strategies we are mindfully remaining in the moment, even when faced with unpleasant and overwhelming feelings. This is hugely empowering and allows us to take a more proactive, courageous role in the moment-to-moment unfolding of our lives. No longer mere backseat passengers unconsciously or unwillingly along for the ride, we climb into the driver's seat, grab the wheel, and steer in a more intentional direction for our lives.

There are only two ways to live your life. One is as though nothing is a miracle. The other is as though everything is a miracle.

—Albert Einstein

The Step Out of Autopilot Mindful Break: Notice when you have been operating on autopilot. Pause and bring your attention to your breath. Observe a few inhales and exhales. Now ask yourself if there is anything you may be avoiding by visiting that virtual reality. It may be that your mind simply slipped off into that virtual reality for no reason other than that is what our minds do constantly. You may occasionally realize, however, that you have hit upon an important discovery. If we are honest with ourselves, it can be a powerful exercise in self-awareness. You need not immediately have all the solutions if some change is required in your life. We must first open up to the recognition of what we are avoiding before anything can be done about it. This is a crucial first step. If this exercise has brought up some uncomfortable feelings, see the Unpleasant Moments Mindful Break (pages 214–15) to learn more. Congratulate yourself for creating the brief time and space to listen to your own wisdom.

The Powerful Pause

My ideal vacation consists of rising without an (electronic or child) alarm, meditating, and enjoying coffee and breakfast before heading out for the day's adventure of hiking, biking, or kayaking. I love to return bone-tired, sweat dried from a day out in nature; shower; relax a bit before a dinner accompanied by a glass of wine or local microbrew; take a trip to the local ice-cream shop; do some reading; and off to bed we go. Rinse and repeat. This may sound terribly dull to some, but to me it is a little slice of heaven.

In the past few years, the daily vacation schedule included somewhat of an enforced midday rest period for us all, as our toddler still required a solid two-hour nap in order to maintain his composure and, consequently, our sanity. Aware we would not be spending an entire day hiking the most challenging trail or biking up the most epic mountain, this quiet time was initially accepted as a necessary inconvenience suffered for the greater good. Instead, it became a lesson in the beauty of slowing down even further. What an unexpected gift.

So, after my little guy laid his curly-haired head down for an afternoon nap, I did something radically different—I paused. I observed my body, my heart, and my mind. I noticed what was called for in those few hours of quiet. How did I really want to spend the time? A restful nap, exploring the nearby shore with my daughter, an uninterrupted chat with my husband, time to read, or to simply sit and daydream as I watched the breeze blowing gently through the trees?

It took a few days, but I slowly felt my body unwind, my muscles breathing a sigh of relief for the rest; not rest in the way of atrophy or disuse, but in the deliberate, relaxed way of mindful movement, exercise, and calm. My pace slowed, my breath slowed, my mind cleared, and I reconnected more deeply with how I want to live my life: being even more mindful of the simple pleasures, including the gift of rest.

While first learning to meditate, people often comment how much easier it is to focus and practice in my office than it is at home. At home, countless distractions clamor for our attention. The same is true with pausing and slowing down. It is much easier to slow the pace on vacation than at home in the midst of chaos and normalcy. But it can be done.

The key is to pause and be still in order to hear the voice inside that is yearning for more play, more rest, and more mindful living of our days. It informs our decisions in a way that is impossible if we never slow down to listen. We then are able to step out of our automatic conditioning, able to hear the judging voice and assess what is needed, what is wanted, and what may ultimately be unnecessary. We all need some time and space to open up to renewed vitality and creativity. It is a practice. It is a choice. We can set the pace of our moments, our days, and our lives.

> Mindfulness does not give us all the answers, but allows us to better hear the questions.
>
> —*Shauna Shapiro*

The Powerful Pause Mindful Break: Pause throughout the day and bring your awareness to the pace you have set, assess its helpfulness, and, if needed, decelerate. Pause and give yourself permission to rest despite the endless list of to-do's. It may mean stepping away from the computer for a moment to stretch or actually taking a half-hour nap, if circumstances allow. The Powerful Pause can help pull us out of our unconscious, habitual way of operating and remind us to pay attention. Offer yourself more permission to simply be, to ease up on the to-do list, and enjoy the little daily pleasures.

Body Scan

There are some folks who are highly aware of their ever-changing body sensations, innately able to recognize and name them. The ability to detect our internal bodily state, called *interoception,* includes the senses of pain, temperature, itch, sensual touch, hunger, thirst, and muscular and organ sensations.

My daughter happens to have a high level of interoception. This natural awareness has its pros and cons but is mostly beneficial. For example, she can recognize the symptoms of a migraine just beginning to form, therefore often averting a full-blown, debilitating one with preventive medication. The downside is that she feels the sensations (including the migraine) more intensely than someone else might. This also means she has a harder time toughing things out. It became clear to me when she was just a little girl that she had a strong sense of interoception when she began describing body sensations in detail, unprompted.

Let me share a few examples. As a long-time bibliophile, I looked forward to the day when my young daughter would read on her own, hoping and imagining she would carry on the avid literary habit. As a toddler, she would pick up as many books as her little arms could carry, drop them in a pile at my feet, and urge me in that sweet two-year-old voice to, "Wead, pwease." I was more than happy to oblige.

Because she was still fairly young and I had not yet made any real attempt to teach her how to read, I was caught off guard the first time I realized she was beginning to read on her own. Perched on my lap at breakfast while I was perusing the morning newspaper, she started to point out various words, reading them aloud. My jaw dropped in delighted surprise. "You can read!" She seemed as excited as me and took off happily reading whatever simple material she could find. When I told her how proud I was of her she grinned ear-to-ear and said, "Mommy, when you say that it makes my belly tickle!"

Another time when she was just a preschooler, we were talking about how she feels when she's misbehaved. Without missing a beat she described how her stomach feels wavy and hurts. I told her how great it was that she is able to notice these body sensations, and she countered, "Mommy, this feeling in my belly is *big*—anyone would notice it!" I'm not so sure about that.

You see, there are many of us for whom body awareness might as well be a foreign language. Depending on your personality, upbringing, and genetics, you may be anywhere on the continuum of hyperaware of body sensations to barely knowing when your hair is on fire. And, of course, our culture supports the yes-I-am-in-pain-but-let's-ignore-this-and-push-through-anyway approach. It's helpful to know and own where you tend to reside on the continuum. As is often the case, somewhere in the middle is typically the most healthy and useful.

If you are highly interoceptive, your goal will be working on noticing, naming, and relaxing around the intense sensations you perceive rather than encouraging increased subtle awareness. The rest of us can benefit from learning to heighten our awareness of body sensations. The good news is that our power of observation can grow with mindfulness practice.

Interoception also includes the awareness of what is commonly referred to as a gut feeling. How many times have you heard someone tell you to trust your gut? For those of us who are challenged with interoception, this is the equivalent to telling someone in the middle of a panic attack to simply calm down. It's not so simple. We need to be taught. But when we learn to tune in to our various inner body sensations, including that perceived gut feeling, it offers us wisdom, not only for what these body sensations may be conveying (*Ah, there is that little twinge of pain in my back—I need to be mindful of how I pick up the laundry basket.*) but also information for what choices to make (While visiting various preschools to find the best fit for your child, you may come upon one that just feels right and one that does not. You may not be able to put your finger on it. Usually that is your gut talking.).

Now that my daughter is older, I hope she notices that wavy discomfort in her belly as a sign she might be about to make a poor choice, heeds it, and changes course, even when it's difficult. This is invaluable when it comes to peer pressure (for both kids and parents). For moms, this can be a helpful barometer when it comes to keeping our level of busyness and stress in check.

Because interoception is not a skill often taught, many of us are completely unaware of how stress is manifesting in body sensations until it becomes obvious and undeniable. Stress can slowly creep up on us, and seemingly out of nowhere we are suffering from chronic headaches, stomach ailments, lowered immune function, painful muscle tightness. The more attentive we are to our bodies, the more we notice subtle changes as they occur and the more we can care for ourselves with wise choices. The Body Scan Mindful Break teaches us to slow down and deliberately notice body sensations as they arise and change. It can also be wonderfully calming and rejuvenating.

The Body Scan Mindful Break: If possible, lie down on a comfortable surface, perhaps covering yourself with a blanket as the body tends to cool a bit in stillness. This mindful break can also be done sitting, standing, or with eyes open throughout the day, although I encourage you to try it first lying down. We ideally want to remain awake for the body scan, so if you are in danger of falling asleep, you may want to keep your eyes open. Otherwise, allow your eyes to close.

Take a few slow, deep breaths in and out. Let your whole body relax and sink into the bed, couch, or floor. Beginning with the feet, notice body sensations that are present, both pronounced and subtle. As you bring curiosity to the body, see if you can also let go and relax those body parts in which you might be holding tension. Don't worry if it's sometimes difficult to identify a sensation or an area that feels neutral; you will notice more subtle sensations with practice. Spend a few seconds on each body part as you slowly scan up the body, bringing your full attention to ankles, lower legs, knees, upper legs, pelvis, hips, bottom, lower back, and so on until you reach the scalp. After you scan through each part, notice the body in its entirety. Relax and let go of any remaining tightness. Perhaps acknowledge and thank your body for how it serves you as you slowly make your way off the bed and bring this more relaxed, body-conscious awareness to the next part of your day. Check in every so often to notice body sensations. Be curious about that gut feeling. When you begin to pay attention, you will inevitably gain some information. Trust it and use it wisely.

SNAP Break

Had you searched for me last night after dinner, you would have found me sitting in the dark shadows of my closet, not exactly hiding from my family but rather taking what I have dubbed a SNAP break.

Thirty minutes prior, I had come home from a long work meeting nursing a headache and feeling overwhelmed with deadlines to face the chaos of my kids joyfully shrieking and running laps inside the house. Had I been in a different mindset, I would have relished the liveliness. Not tonight. Cringing at the volume, I felt thoughts begin to swirl in my head and impatience rise inside like a storm. If I didn't do something to change course, I was sure to snap, transforming from Mindful Mommy to Mommy Dearest right before their eyes. Oh, I have attempted in the past to muscle through this impending feeling with mostly disastrous results. I knew from experience that we are all much better off if I head straight for the closet for a little respite. Rather than snap, I took a SNAP Break:

Stop, Notice, Accept, and Pay attention to your breath.

So into the closet I went, among the clothes and wire hangers—nothing magical about this place save its solitude and quiet. I took a SNAP Break to spare myself, my husband, my children, and the dog from a mama on the verge of losing it.

> Parenting is a mirror in which we get to see the best of ourselves, and the worst; the richest moments of living, and the most frightening.
>
> *—Myla and Jon Kabat-Zinn*

We aren't always able to physically step away from stressful situations, but if we are familiar with the SNAP Break, we can learn to use it anywhere, anytime. It takes practice, patience, and above all, some self-forgiveness when Mommy Dearest appears in spite of our best efforts.

As for this stressed mama, when I emerged from my brief retreat, the threat of Mommy Dearest remained tucked away safely in the closet with the wire hangers. Mindful Mommy was back and ready to be with, really *be with*, my family again, my attitude adjusted, a larger perspective regained, all recovered with a quick SNAP Break.

The SNAP Mindful Break: Stop. Hit the pause button. If possible, step away for a moment. Notice your body sensations. Are your shoulders raised? Is your brow furrowed? Your jaw tight? Your breath shallow? Accept that this is how it is in this moment. Offer yourself some compassion. Pay attention to the breath for a moment, simply noticing as it comes and goes, without trying to change it. When your mind wanders to the stresses at hand, gently redirect your attention back to the breath. Repeat as needed.

CHAPTER 2

Starting Your Day

It's early Monday morning, and my eyes barely opened slits as I sense the radiance of warm sunshine from my bedroom windows. Through a haze of sleepiness I wonder why it seems much brighter than usual for a typical weekday, pre-alarm. I peer over at my ancient clock radio, my brain slowly registering with dismay that I have overslept by an entire sixty minutes. Grumbling a string of inappropriate choice words, I throw off the covers and leap out of bed.

Adrenaline surging, heart racing, I run to wake my daughter, let the dog out, and make my way to the coffeemaker. Rushing around, I spill the milk, curse again, and will myself to take a few deep(er) breaths. I shower without any memory of shampooing, my mind frantically focused on what needs to get done if I'm to make it to work on time.

Wrestling my toddler into his clothes (comparable to wrestling an unwilling gator), I hastily offer a single blue M&M used as guilty bribery for potty training. He savors it like a lollipop, bright blue drool covering his hands, mouth, and shirt. I decide whoever is responsible for designing such vividly clothes-staining M&M hues is clearly not a parent of young children, and I curse that person, too.

Changing my toddler (again) out of his blue-stained clothes, I manage to get my daughter to the bus stop. My son, the dog, and

I are out the door on time, in record time, and I finally take a few full breaths as I merge onto the highway.

Whoa, that was exhausting, I think. I drop my shoulders and breathe more deeply, which my son then dramatically imitates from the backseat. I chuckle, begin to relax, and as I slowly come back to my senses realize just how unnecessarily frenzied the past hour has been.

And in that moment of settling down, I notice the glaring disparity between this morning and one after which I've taken time to meditate. The juxtaposition between the two is an apt analogy for how I had been living versus what it's like to live mindfully: frantic versus calm, autopilot versus savoring moments, grinding along on the unending hamster wheel versus keeping a measured, stress-free pace.

Dr. Richard J. Davidson and Sharon Begley report in their book, *The Emotional Life of Your Brain*:

> Mindfulness trains the brain in new forms of responding to experience and thoughts. Whereas the thought of how much you need to accomplish tomorrow... used to trigger a panicky sense of being overwhelmed, mindfulness sends thoughts through a new culvert: You still think about all you have to do, but when the sense of being overwhelmed

> kicks in, you regard that thought with dispassion. . . . You step back from it and let it go, realizing that allowing it to hijack your brain won't help. Mindfulness retrains these habits of mind by tapping into the plasticity of the brain's connections, creating new ones, strengthening some old ones, and weakening others.

Mindfulness is not magic. It does not remove the blue stain from the clothing or the spilled milk from the counter, but when practiced regularly it does shift our perspective from urgent and frantic to inconvenient and not life altering. And no matter how much mindfulness I practice, those brightly dyed M&M's? Still not a fan.

Waking with Gratitude

For years after becoming a mom, waking up in the morning would typically go something like this: Thought #1: *What is that hideous noise?* Thought #2: *Damn. Alarm. Already?* #3: *I am so tired. I hate being tired. Never enough sleep. . . .*

These days, depending upon the circumstances, thoughts 1 to 3 may still arise. After all, as moms we certainly don't always

The thought manifests as the word;
The word manifests as the deed;
The deed develops into habit;
And habit hardens into character.
So watch the thought and its ways with care,
And let it spring from love,
Born out of compassion for all human beings.
As the shadow follows the body,
As we think, so we become.

—*Sayings of the Buddha as cited by Das*

have control of our sleep. We also don't have control over which thoughts show up, only over what we choose to do with those thoughts. With mindfulness practice, I have now learned to notice those thoughts and then choose instead to shift my focus and wake with gratitude, appreciating the positive tone it sets for the day.

The Waking with Gratitude Mindful Break: As soon as you are conscious enough to realize you are awake(ish), pause and take a deep breath. (At first, this may not be until you have stumbled out of bed to attend to a child or poured your first cup of coffee. That's fine; pause wherever you are. After practicing for a bit, you will catch yourself sooner, before you make your way out of bed.) Bring to mind those things for which you are grateful. Perhaps it is your health, your children, your partner, friends, coffee, birds singing, sun shining, rain falling. Keep it simple and keep it positive. Throughout your day take note of how this mindfulness shifts your perception of those things normally taken for granted into a greater sense of appreciation.

Coffee

Before the arrival of my little guy four years ago, I was a reasonably well-rested human being who meditated for thirty minutes early each morning. After rousing to my pre-dawn alarm, I would shuffle to the bathroom, splash some shockingly cold (but oddly pleasant) water on my face, and soon be fairly awake and alert. On the occasional sleepy morning the fantasy of some pre-meditation coffee would arise, but I never actually indulged. The rule-follower in me would have surely chastised loudly: *What would the great meditation teachers think of that? Tsk, tsk.* And so, regardless of my level of sleepiness, for better or worse I sat for thirty decaffeinated minutes, making a beeline straight to my beloved coffeemaker as soon as that half hour was up.

Confession time: My morning meditation has changed somewhat since that time. My older, and questionably wiser, self has taken to breaking this rule on occasion, often with a hint of rebellion (I did say *hint*, progress for someone usually so compliant). I broke the rule initially by necessity, but now I do it purely because I enjoy the habit. Yes, I often meditate while savoring my cup of coffee. I love the stuff. It may have saved my life on numerous occasions. In my estimation, it certainly deserves a meditation dedicated solely to its lovely qualities.

> Drink your tea slowly and reverently, as if it is the axis on which the world earth revolves—slowly, evenly, without rushing toward the future; live the actual moment. Only this moment is life.
>
> *–Thich Nhat Hanh*

Whether you are a java aficionado like me or a tea lover, you can practice the Coffee Mindful Break with your caffeinated or decaffeinated beverage of choice. (Though I don't recommend wine in the morning. The Wine Mindful Break (pages 233–34) comes later. Be patient, my friend.)

The Coffee Mindful Break: A note of caution: Before you settle in and sit down in a haze of sleepy fog, take note of where you place your cup so as not to spill all over the floor when you complete the mindful break. Trust me on this one.

Sit tall in a comfortable position, either in a chair or on a cushion on the floor. Holding your cup in both hands, feel the warmth radiating into your hands, feel the smooth or coarse texture of the mug. Slowly lift the mug to your nose and inhale the scent as if for the first time. Without judgment, notice what thoughts arise.

Notice how the muscles in your arms know just what to do as they lift the cup to your mouth.

Despite the urge to ingest the caffeine as soon as humanly possible (sounds a little desperate, but I've been there), see if you can pause for a moment and observe what happens. Is your mouth watering in sweet anticipation? Are your thoughts screaming for you to *please take a giant swig already*? Just notice. Then, with deliberate action, place the cup to your lips. Now, take that first glorious sip and hold the flavorful liquid in your mouth, tasting as fully as you can. As you swallow, experience the warmth moving its way down your throat and into your stomach. Pause. Take a breath before your next sip. As you do, notice what occurs in the body. Has your heart rate increased? Does your mind feel more alert? Are the sensations pleasant or unpleasant? Tuning into our body sensations offers us subtle information we might otherwise miss. Perhaps you relish the mental sharpness that occurs. Perhaps you realize the caffeine causes slight feelings of anxiety and you decide to live without. These sensations and reactions may also shift over time. Keep watching. Stay curious. Enjoy.

Showering

I think I shampooed my hair twice in the shower this morning. I say *I think* because I'm still not sure. I'm not sure because my mind was not in the shower with me, but at work with patients, with my daughter at school, and at the grocery store with the future contents of my fridge. Slipping into autopilot can occur in the strangest of places. It happens to all of us—it's part of the human condition. Even when we are reasonably on our game our minds wander, but it's especially likely when it comes to an activity as routine as showering.

For most of us, the novelty of the bathtub has long since worn off, but if you are the mom of a newborn (or remember back to when you were), a shower may seem like a major coup and not something easily taken for granted. You may notice and appreciate every detail from the hot, soothing

Most people don't realize that the mind constantly chatters. And yet, that chatter winds up being the force that drives us much of the day in terms of what we do, what we react to, and how we feel.

—Jon Kabat-Zin

water to the delightful scent of shampoo and soap. And if you get lucky enough (or care enough at this stage of the game) to have time to shave your legs, well, you might just think you've died and gone straight to heaven.

Once our wee ones fall into a rhythm, the shower once again becomes mundane. It's no longer a major accomplishment for the day and often a time when we mentally scroll through our to-do lists and zone out. Use this mindful break to bring back a bit of that long-ago appreciation.

The Showering Mindful Break: As best you can, bring your full awareness to each step in showering. As you turn on the faucet and wait for the water to reach the right temperature, take a few long, deep breaths. You might offer gratitude for the mere appearance of water with one rotation of the faucet, an unheard of luxury for some in our world. Be as aware of body sensations as possible as you allow the water to cascade over your hair and down your body. Beginning with the scalp, slowly scan down the body, pausing for a few seconds in each area to notice sensations. When your mind wanders off, notice where it went and redirect your attention back to the body. Breathe in the fragrance of soap and shampoo. If the shower is something you typically rush through, decelerate the pace just a tad. I promise you won't miss those lost thirty seconds.

Regardless of your current relationship with your body, I invite you to offer appreciation for it as you towel off—appreciation for its strength, its beauty, and its amazing ability to function as it does. This is the body that nurtures and cares for your babies—whether your babies are new or fully grown. We tend to feel innate warmth toward those who show care for our children. My guess is you are the one who cares the most, and therefore, by default you deserve your own compassionate admiration.

Breakfast

I have a longstanding habit of reading while eating breakfast. As a kid I remember perusing the local newspaper while munching on Froot Loops (don't judge; this was the early eighties, people). I still enjoy the weekend paper or online blogs with my morning bagel with almond butter and banana. Some days while engrossed in an article, I may eventually gaze down at my empty plate with very little recollection of having eaten. So every few days I set the paper and computer aside and savor a mindful breakfast.

The Breakfast Mindful Break: Try eating a mindful breakfast once a week. Close the computer, put away your phone, and turn off the TV. If you are eating with your family, invite them to do the same. Bring your full focus to the food and your senses. Take a moment to reflect on the food itself. What did it take to get breakfast to your plate? Where did the food grow? Did it need to be transported? Purchased? Prepared? Look at the food as if you have never seen it before. What do you notice about the color, texture, shape, and size? Use your sense of smell to detect hints of sweetness, spice, or earthiness. Bring the food to your lips, perhaps noticing increased salivation as you do. Place the first bite of food in your mouth and without chewing take note of flavors. Eat the first few bites more slowly, continuing with this feast for your senses. When your mind wanders, gently bring it back to the food and your Breakfast Mindful Break. If you take your time, you may notice that less food is needed for you to feel satiated. Mindful eating reminds us to honor our bodies and level of true hunger; it often leads to healthier, more enjoyable eating habits.

Brushing Teeth

Some years back I taught eight-week Mindfulness-Based Stress Reduction courses at my local hospital. Part of students' home practice included identifying what is called a mindful bell, or one daily routine that served as a reminder to bring their full attention to it each time it occurred. Often, I would name brushing my teeth, since it was an ongoing challenge for me to remain present during this two-minute activity. To this day, I find it amusing how challenging it is for me to stay still while brushing my teeth. There seems to be some innate force compelling me to walk around, desperately looking to multitask. Perhaps it is due to boredom, a long-held belief that I am wasting precious time, or purely out of habit. Whatever the cause, I have learned to notice the pull to move and gently will myself to stay put, but even many years later it is rarely easy.

I shouldn't be surprised, then, that my little guy has inherited the same tooth-brushing wanderlust as his mom, maddening for me as this often is—a double standard, I know. I place that toothbrush in his little hand and he instantly heads out of the bathroom to explore the contents of my closet or putter with any potential distraction on his meandering path.

When crunched for time, I may chase him around, hypocritically muttering, "Please come here. Come back here. Can't you just stay put?" On a more mindful day, however, I take a deep breath, steer him back to the bathroom, and smile—brushing teeth just may be his lifelong mindful bell practice as well. Seems the roaming apple doesn't fall far from the tree.

Research also shows that too much multitasking has the same effect on our IQs as a bong hit. It makes us do stupid things. And yet, life with young children often requires an absurd, stuntman level of multitasking—something we do more than half our waking time.

—Katrina Alcorn

The Brushing Teeth Mindful Break: Allow brushing your teeth to become a mindful bell while you spend those requisite two minutes polishing your smile. Notice where your thoughts are as you begin a habit so ingrained that it can be easily glossed over. Perhaps set a timer for two minutes and with amusement count how many times your mind slips off the task and needs to be redirected. It's amazing how our minds so often resemble busy toddlers jumping from one activity to the next. Gently yet firmly redirect your attention, just as you would your children. Challenge yourself to be fully present by paying attention to the minty smell and tingly sensation in your mouth. Notice the amount of pressure you apply as you brush, and see if you can lighten it a bit. When your timer rings, offer yourself a smile in the mirror and show off your work. Perhaps set an intention to share your smile with whomever you encounter throughout the day.

The To-Do List

Time is so capricious. Slow, fast, elusive—all depending upon the circumstances of the moment. When I sit at my computer to write, time slips away in hour-long increments. I look up from the screen and two hours have passed in what feels like the span of a few brief minutes. Unfortunately for both my son and me, assembling Legos seems to have the opposite effect on me, slowing my perception of time to a painful crawl. Sorry, little guy.

My impression of time is also affected by what I have placed on my daily to-do list. I love lists because they allow me to transfer the seemingly infinite minutiae taking up precious real estate in my mind to a tangible piece of paper, thereby relieving me of the effort required to retain it all. The to-do list also dramatically decreases the chance of random items popping into my head while drifting off to sleep, causing me to bolt upright with an *Oh, %$#, I forgot to call so-and-so!* The fewer times that happens, the better.

Oh, but there is so much to remember. There is the master list, which is the repository for all I wish not to forget, and the daily list, containing those items to be completed that day. Why so much emphasis on lists? Because, among the copious roles we moms play, most of us are also the managers of our homes. Different from wearing the family pants (although we may do that, too), the manager is in charge of the incessant details that take up so much headspace. Birthdays, carpool, dentist appointments, school forms, vitamins, fund-raisers, playdates, sports schedules, babysitting schedules . . . on and on it goes. This is no small thing, the tremendous time and effort involved.

> In pursuit of knowledge, every day something is acquired. In pursuit of wisdom, every day something is dropped.
>
> *—Lao Tzu*

Most early mornings after meditating and my beloved cup of coffee, you can find me constructing my list for the day. As I write, I am also vaguely aware that when the caffeine buzz wears off and reality sets in, I will often have to adjust the ambitiousness of the list. On those days when I don't pause to assess the true feasibility of the list, I feel especially time starved and stressed, unwittingly setting myself up to feel as if there is not enough time in the day to accomplish it all (because there simply isn't). I scramble around completing tasks at a slightly frantic pace, not fully aware of what I am doing, finishing one task while mentally preparing for the next. When I don't stop to take a few deep breaths, I may regard what has arbitrarily been written on the list as the law—as in, *this must get done today or else.* Or else what?

Since having kids, often I also try to squeeze in just one more thing before needing to be somewhere. Occasionally more is accomplished, but at what cost? Yes, there can be a bit of a pleasant adrenaline rush that comes from crossing things off the list, but I have found ways to tweak this frenetic pace, actually rendering me more productive while simultaneously seeming to slow time. Our experience of time passing can be considerably influenced by the pace at which we move, both in body and mind, and the sense of urgency behind it.

Sure, there are some items that must be taken care of today. Most, however, will still be there when we get to them because, in reality, the list is endless. As counterintuitive as it sounds, I have found it immensely helpful *not* to squeeze in that one extra thing. When I whittle down the daily list, it is amazing how my pace no longer feels urgent, how my sense of time becomes one of plenty. Because there *is* plenty of time. And those items on the list? They are all eventually crossed off, inevitably soon to be replaced by more.

The To-Do List Mindful Break: First pause and take a few deep, mindful breaths. As you examine your to-do list, notice what arises in your body. Do you feel a sense of butterflies in the stomach? Tightness in the shoulders? Are you feeling overwhelmed? Perhaps you have constructed a reasonable list for the day and your body feels relaxed, your mind is at ease, and you have a sense of excitement for the day. This pausing and noticing enables us to prioritize and let go, if needed, of what is not absolutely necessary. Take care with turning items on your list into facts. Ask yourself if each task is a true requirement for the day.

It is quite challenging to live mindfully when we are rushing from one thing to the next. If possible, place a few things into the *if there is time* category, or take a few items off the list completely, thereby allowing yourself a little more space in your day to move at a steady, mindful pace. Do this every day for a week and notice how much you have accomplished and with what level of awareness. Adjust each day as necessary.

The Bus Stop

I still remember the early morning of my daughter's first day of kindergarten—the anticipated uncertainty of how I would react when she stepped onto the bus and waved good-bye from the window. Would I be one of the wistful mamas wiping away tears or one of the giddy moms jumping for joy? As I recall, it was some combination of the two. I felt both a sigh of nostalgic recognition for this new chapter in her life and gratitude for a few fleeting hours of alone time. I remember, after watching the school bus pull away with my precious cargo, distractedly completing some chores at home, anticipating her return, and being curious about how the first day had been. I imagined the excitement, nervousness, and wonder she must have been experiencing.

A few long-lasting hours later I was relieved to see my little girl spring off that bus with a smile, excitedly sharing how she had sat with a new friend both to and from school on the bus. "She looks just like me, Mom! She has light brown hair, blue eyes, and chubby cheeks!" From the mouth of babes directly to tears in my eyes (*there* was the delayed reaction I had anticipated).

We settled into the school routine, the seasons passed, and the bus stop's climate, both in real and emotional weather, changed over time as well. There were tearful times when my daughter was the target of subversive girl bullying, excited times for a field trip, nervous times before a big presentation, and calm times when things seemed to be rolling along smoothly and with ease.

But, oh, how the bus-stop rituals have shifted over those years since kindergarten. During the sweet first years of elementary school there were hugs and kisses and I love you's as the bus rolled to a stop in front of us. Enthusiastic waves and air kisses were engaged in by all as the bus slowly pulled away. The later elementary years permitted a one-armed *this-is-slightly-embarrassing-but-I-will-relent* hug and a warm but not too enthusiastic parting wave meant to appear sort of cool, much like the preteen herself.

In middle school and beyond, absolutely no waving, no touching, and, for the love of God, no expression of affection whatsoever is tolerated. Which, of course, is an open invitation to heap on the hugs and affection for the pure embarrassment factor my daughter grudgingly endures (which I do only on the first day of school—I do have *some* compassion, after all). As a mother to a teen, I have come to find a bit of twisted pleasure in the harmless embarrassment I can bestow. I am *so* not cool, but it sure is fun. (And, by the way, despite our moving to a new school district a few years into elementary school, the two first-day chubby-cheeked seatmates are now beautiful, bright teens and close friends to this day.)

Mindful Bus Stop Break: Whatever the schooling stage, whatever the age of your kids, *be there,* whether it seems to matter to them or not. Put the cell phone down—perhaps even leave it at home. Be ready for any last-minute conversation, meaningful look, or last-chance glance for reassurance. Think of it as shoring them up for the day out in the big, wide world—a world that can be trying or benevolent depending on the day. If you are so inclined, say a silent loving wish or prayer for your child as he makes his way up those bus steps. He's already carrying your heart, so go ahead and send some warm wishes right along with him as well.

CHAPTER 3

Connecting with Your Family During the Day

Once upon a time I awoke each morning before my daughter, my husband, and the sun to meditate for thirty continuous, peaceful moments. Only on the rarest of occasions was this time interrupted by the outside world or my little slumbering family. As is always the case with meditation, my mind drifted off countless times in those thirty minutes, but I could almost guarantee that no one in my home would voluntarily stir at such an ungodly hour. And so for that much-loved half hour it was just me, myself, my wandering thoughts, and I. Quiet. Calm. Consistent.

Then my son was born. Cue the ear-piercing sound of the old record player needle screeching across vinyl. Good-bye, meditation as I once knew it. Hello, new normal.

Take this morning, for example. It's a bit after 5 AM and I am sitting in the hushed darkness of our living room, the crickets outside and the dog by my side my only companions. As I settle in to notice the steady inhale and exhale of my breath—in, out, in, out—I'm startled to hear a tiny yet mighty voice yell from the upstairs bedroom, "Hello . . . ? Hello . . . ? I'm firsty . . . I'm firsty!" I sigh as I heave myself up off the floor and my meditation cushion.

My little guy would love to begin his day now, but it is entirely too early. To buy myself some time, I move swiftly up the stairs, sit down on his bed, place him tenderly on my lap, and pop the milk-filled sippy cup squarely in his mouth. He relaxes back against my chest, contentedly drinking away.

If I were a beginning meditator, this interruption would've caused me great frustration, as in, *he ruined my precious half hour!* Likewise, it is common for beginners to think there is some sought-after perfect meditation. Not so. Each meditation is how it is that day—peaceful or anxiety ridden, sleepy or restless, or all of the above.

It has taken some time, but I have learned to allow, and even relax into, these imperfect moments. I still prefer the uninterrupted time, but now this time with my boy becomes my practice. Meditation is kindly training our minds to repeatedly come back to the present moment, accepting whatever arises. Our children can be our greatest teachers, if we allow them.

Snuggled up on the bed with my boy, I gently pull myself out of my thoughts and notice what is (literally) right in front of me. I sense the weight of his muscular little body on my lap. I place my hand on his birdlike rib cage, feeling the strong beat of the heart that has stolen mine. I notice his warmth, the still baby-like softness of the skin as I caress his face. I hold that tiny hand in mine and am in awe of those small, lovely fingers. He gently grips my hand, and my heart swells. I notice my breath—in, out, in, out.

I imagine the future when there will be no interruptions, bittersweet in its peacefulness. But for now, it is silent. I am here. After all, no meditation is perfect. Some are decidedly less so. And some, my friends, are downright heavenly.

Start small and start now. Let go of expectations and preconceived notions. Embrace the messiness of this life, in all its imperfection. Sometimes that is precisely where the biggest gifts reside.

Whether you are expecting your first baby (Congratulations; get ready for the most rewarding journey of your life!) or your fifth grandbaby, you will find simple ways here to immerse your family's life in more calm, connection, and balance. The following mindful breaks will help you find the joy in parenting and connecting to your family. They also will help you connect to yourself—your own needs and well-being, both vital to happy families.

Raising Happiness author Christine Carter shares this research:

> Practicing mindfulness doesn't just lead to decreased stress and increased pleasure in parenting, it brings profound benefits to kids [even if it is only the parents that are practicing]. Parents who practiced mindful parenting skills for a year were dramatically more satisfied with their parenting skills and their interactions with their children, even though no new parenting practices beyond being mindful had been taught to them. Over the course of the year-long study, the behavior of these mindful parents' kids also changed for the better: they got along better with their siblings and were less aggressive, and their social skills improved. And all their parents did was practice mindfulness.

I have seen mindfulness transform the lives of moms in all stages of parenting. Take those practical five minutes and let it do the same for you. The mindful breaks in this chapter will allow you to creatively and seamlessly incorporate mindfulness into your family's life—whether feeding your newborn, sharing an after-school snack with your preteen, or facing your teen's increasing desire for independence, there are mindful breaks designed to help you cope with the challenges and savor the blessings.

The Three-Breath Hug

I learned this practice when my daughter was a preschooler and taught it to her with the intention of using it as a sweet way to calm her emotional outbursts. As is often the case with parenting, I mistakenly thought I was the wise one offering something for her benefit until she astutely reversed the plan, reminding me just how much I learn from her.

> When you hold a child in your arms, or hug your mother, or your husband, or your friend, if you breathe in and out three times, your happiness will be multiplied at least tenfold.
>
> —*Thich Nhat Hanh*

One particularly stressful evening I had retreated to the bathroom for a much-needed mommy time-out, closing my eyes and taking a number of deep breaths. Hearing a scuffling sound outside the door, I opened my eyes to see a folded piece of paper slid under the door. Unfolding it, my heart warmed with love as I read the message written in that adorable five-year-old scrawl: "Meet me in my room for a 3 breth hug."

The Three-Breath Hug Mindful Break: While hugging your child, take three deliberate, synchronized, deep breaths together. Drop your shoulders and relax any muscles that feel tight. Let go and feel the tension melt away. Teach the hug to your kids and your partner. Little ones love it and teenagers secretly do, too. Use it as you say good-bye in the morning, when you recognize that your child could use a calming hug, or just for the love of it. You never know when they will surprise you and offer a much-needed three-breath hug to dear old Mom.

Your Teen Driver

Can you recall gently buckling your astonishingly tiny newborn in the car seat for his first trip home from the hospital? *Blink.* How about looking into your rearview mirror at your backward-facing infant's reflection (complete with pacifier-filled mouth) in the mirror strategically strapped across the backseat? *Blink.* Remember craning your neck to quickly steal a glance at his beaming toddler smile while you sang together with abandon? *Blink.* How about the chatty preschool years when he didn't seem to take a breath between an unending string of sentences and you longed for the briefest respite of silence? *Blink.* Now you look sideways and his long legs are stretched out in the passenger seat next to you, his solid forearm slightly touching yours on the center armrest. Oh, and there is that silence you once longed for—perpetual earbuds have taken care of that and, in fact, it is often now *too* quiet. *Blink.* You are now in the passenger seat as your teen sits impossibly grown next to you in the driver's seat. How did this happen? You blinked, and here you are. Now what?

As far as I have come in my mothering journey, I am not here yet. I have a few more years to blink before my daughter reaches this teenage rite of passage. As it moves ever closer, I am surprised to find that I don't dread it, presumably because my girl has grown into a cautiously astute, responsible young woman. But, of course, that is her. Mostly I fear the other distracted drivers on the road. As her time to drive nears, those impending worries will arise, and I imagine it will be an ongoing piece of my mindfulness practice to work with them. As the saying goes, once we have kids, it's like we forever have our hearts vulnerably walking around outside our bodies. Ultimately, though, I take solace in the belief that after my girl learns how to operate a vehicle, she will be an excellent, safe driver.

Teaching her to drive, well, that is another story altogether. That image strikes a bit of terror in my heart. Fortunately, my loving teen has already informed me that it will be her father, not me, who is the chosen instructor. I am more than OK with it mostly because I doubt my level of patience for this significant undertaking. Come to think of it, I was too impatient to teach her to tie her shoes. There *are* certain situations in which I can exhibit the utmost patience. I fear this may not be one of them.

Not to mention, I don't really enjoy fearing for my life. I love to bike, but never down a mountain. I love to swan dive off the diving board into the cool swimming pool water, but never from the high board. I like a bit of adventure in my life, but mostly I like to play it safe. And remain uninjured. And alive.

So, yes, my husband is welcome to instruct. I am aware that this plan could, of course, change. The presumed harmonious combination of my husband and daughter may not go as imagined. I may need to step in. And I will, of course, if necessary. I have talked with friends with older kids about their experience of teaching their teenage children to drive. I have listened and stored away their advice for my own potential future use. And I am pulling it out for this mindful break. So let's both take a big, deep, calming breath before we begin.

The Your Teen Driver Mindful Break: Take that deep inhale and exhale. In fact, take a whole bunch. I think you are going to need them. As you sit shotgun (what?) next to your child, briefly scan your body to notice any areas of tightness. Drop your shoulders, relax your legs, and soften the small muscles around your eyes, brow, and mouth. If your teen is amenable, you may want to suggest she does the same.

As best you can, keep your body relaxed and your tone measured, but don't work so hard trying to appear calm. Your teen is nervous. She knows full well you are, too. Acknowledging and accepting this fact allows us to focus more clearly on the task at hand. Every so often, pause, breathe, and check in with the tension in your body. Relax those muscles. Remind yourself and your child that you are both doing fine.

If tension between the two of you arises, you may want to use the STOP the Teen 'Tude (pages 114–15) or Unpleasant Moments (pages 214–15) Mindful Breaks. It may help to remind yourself that this is a moment to be noticed, perhaps even savored, a memory you might one day relish, even the tough parts. Remember what happened when you blinked before? And, finally, if all else fails, there is always the option of hiring an outside, unbiased driver education teacher. No shame in that. In fact, it may well be worth every last penny, not to mention your precious sanity.

Bottle- or Breast-Feeding

Breast or bottle—as far as I am concerned, whichever is best for you, your baby, your situation, and your sanity is the right decision. Everyone's situation varies from child to child, including mine. I was pleased to be able to successfully breastfeed my daughter but, for numerous reasons, things did not go as smoothly with my son. Whichever you choose (if you are fortunate enough to choose), you are nourishing and nurturing your little babe and will, either way, be spending loads upon loads of time doing so.

The way I see it, feeding our infants is similar to meditation in that, if we sit for more extended periods of time, we may feel alternately bored, blissful, restless, sleepy, content. Depending on the conditions—the time of day, our mood, how new we are to breastfeeding, and how well it is going—we can pass through several of these stages within the course of one feeding. I remember thinking my daughter was attached to my breast throughout the day more often than not (because she probably was). I recall some feeding sessions when I waited impatiently for her to finish. Others were a welcome respite from the outside world, an opportunity to reconnect with this little bundle of wonder, grateful to be fully present for the miracle of it all.

The Bottle- or Breast-Feeding Mindful Break: Notice your mood at the outset of the feeding. Are you feeling peaceful, restless, bored, grateful, resentful? Can you accept without judgment whatever mood shows up? Shift your attention to body sensations. What do you notice? Perhaps it is the warmth of her body against yours, her lips against your nipple, her little body relaxing a bit as she settles in, feeling the tingling of the let-down reflex, your breath, her breath. Observe the miracle of that tiny mouth eager for the bottle, the little swallows and breaths as he receives sustenance. Each time your mind wanders, gently redirect your attention to the many ever-changing body sensations. Let this time be your mindfulness practice. Although often impossible to imagine in the throes of new motherhood, feeding will one day come to an end, and you will look back on it in wonder. Be there, as best you can, in body and in mind.

Lunch

Lunch in our house looks wildly different depending on the day and scheduling circumstances. During the school week, it is just my little guy and me. Although I try to minimize them, there are those days when I feel pressure to shovel some food into his mouth, fill his little belly, and send him off for a nap so I can get to some pressing work phone calls or writing. This usually amounts to both of us eating at the kitchen island, him standing on a chair and me leaning on my elbows next to him, alternately tidying the kitchen, keeping him on task, and picking from his plate. Not exactly a recipe for mindful eating.

Other somewhat more evolved days might find us sitting at the dining room table, where we eat most of our meals, ingesting our lunch like human beings rather than ravenous animals. In typically active four-year-old fashion, this often amounts to a bite or two of food followed by a lap around the inside of the house, repeated until satiated belly has been achieved. This option offers a bit more opportunity for a mindful lunch for Mom, despite its intermittent togetherness.

My favorite lunches, though, take place at the wrought-iron table outside on our patio gazebo, a covered porch overlooking our backyard and view of nearby South Mountain. The table is set into a nook, protected from wind and shaded from sun; you can find us there three seasons out of the year and even on the occasional mild winter day. On a recent chilly fall day, we sat bundled in our winter coats and hats with soup and sandwiches, removing our gloves only to eat.

We both relish the fresh air, changing sights of the seasons, and the conversation that seems to flow more easily as we sit surrounded by Mother Nature. There's something about that special place that encourages my little guy to slow down and eat, seemingly lulled by the expansiveness of the outdoors. It is there where I also feel most relaxed, away from the beckoning emails and phone calls, mostly free of distraction.

The Lunch Mindful Break: Whether you choose the outdoors or not, find a special place in your home to encourage a more mindful lunch. Perhaps an indoor picnic on a soft blanket laid out on the living room floor, a cozy couch in a room free of electronics, outside under a tree, or on a special bench. Create the conditions for a mindful lunch: distraction free, comfortable, and novel. Notice and name what stands out for you. Is it the warmth of the sun, the softness of the blanket, the sound of silence? Take a breath and offer gratitude for the food and the time together. Eat slowly and discuss the flavors, the smells, the textures of the food. This may not happen every day, and that is fine. Let go of expectations, slow down, and have fun with it. Let it become your special mindful lunch ritual.

Just Dance

Music can have such a powerful effect on our moods. Certain songs can pull us right back to a time long ago, evoking associated memories and moods. When my daughter was an infant I had so many nicknames for her that I was concerned she would never learn her own name. One of her nicknames, *Lucy*, also happened to be the name of an upbeat, very danceable Ryan Adams song popular on our local indie radio station at the time. I reminisce about holding her tightly in my arms as we moved to the beat of the fast-paced music, joyful smiles plastered on both our faces, our eyes locking occasionally in glances of mutual love and enjoyment. Some thirteen years later, I can't hear that song without smiling and being flooded with bittersweet memories of a little girl nestled perfectly in my arms.

How we spend our days is, of course, how we spend our lives.
—Annie Dillard

I followed suit with my little guy, finding our favorite danceable tunes both slow and fast. "Roller Coaster" by Kira Willey was our go-to get-our-groove-on song; Red Molly's version of

"May I Suggest" to this day places a lump firmly in my throat and tears well up in my eyes whenever I hear it. It is apparent my little boy still feels it, too. These music-filled memories are precious moments shared between a mom and dear child deeply in sync with each other. It doesn't get much better than that.

The Just Dance Mindful Break: Add some more music to your day. Notice what is called for in the moment. What is the current mood? Could it use a bit of shifting or a bit of enhancing? Pull out some appropriate-to-the-moment music and dance. Perhaps it is an upbeat song full of energy and movement needed to shake off a tantrum or sibling argument. Maybe what is called for is some winding down with a slow dance full of tenderness and love. As you move with your beloved child, notice your body sensations. Are you feeling increased energy throughout your body? Is there a relaxing of your shoulders? A smile on your face? Do you feel warmth in the area of your chest and heart? What about your breath? Has it slowed down or speeded up to keep pace with the music? There is no right or wrong way to Just Dance. Simply be there as fully as possible, giving yourself over to the moment, the music, the movement, the love. Groove on, dear Mama.

Pleasant Moments

There are some early mornings where I find myself lost in thought, planning for the day while eating breakfast with my kids. Although I am physically present and clearly meeting our basic nutritional needs, my mind is nowhere to be found at the dining room table. When I remember to bring my full attention to the moment, using the Triangle of Awareness as a brief guide (thoughts, emotions, and body sensations), I return to the table and am suddenly flooded with love and gratitude for my children. I notice the warmth that fills my heart and the smile that forms on my face as I look into their eyes. In that moment when their eyes meet mine, they know that I am completely there with them. What had one moment earlier been a mundane, neutral moment has been transformed into a lovely one of connection, all with merely a deliberate shifting of my attention.

Life is not a dress rehearsal. Every day, you should have at least one exquisite moment.

—Sally Karioth

The Pleasant Moments Mindful Break: Using the Triangle of Awareness (page 31) as a guide, be on the lookout for at least one pleasant moment each day. When you encounter what seems to be a neutral, easy-to-miss moment, notice your thoughts and the emotions present, and briefly scan through the body for any noticeable sensations. No need to force anything to happen. Accept, as best you can, whatever is revealed—pleasant, unpleasant, or neutral. Simply paying attention may not result in a shift from neutral to pleasant, but it is often a welcome side effect.

Pillow Fight!

I am not a fan of some of the habits we have allowed our little guy to form, such as TV watching upon waking in the morning. I may have initially succumbed to this request because as he watches, he also snuggles up warmly on my lap while I read. It is by far one of my most pleasant times of the day. Yes, I am somewhat shamefully admitting that I am willing to sacrifice a small portion of his young brain cells for my own selfish cuddling pleasure.

Lest you judge my seemingly self-centered parenting choices, one healthier habit I adore is what we have come to call our daily pillow fight, which consists of blaring upbeat music on the ancient clock radio in my bedroom while throwing pillows at each other, dancing, and tickling. Basically, just plain silliness. We both love the belly laughs, the physicality of it, and the few moments of completely being with each other with zero distractions. Our pillow fights have become as routine as brushing our teeth in the morning (in fact, the fun begins right after teeth are cleaned).

If I sense a tantrum heading our way (his or mine), I am also quick to suggest a pillow fight at any time of the day or night. I never cease to be amazed at how the music, dancing, and playfulness can dissipate any sour mood in a matter of moments.

The Pillow Fight! Mindful Break: If anyone's mood could use a little sprucing up (or even if it doesn't), turn up the music and dance with abandon. Remind yourself that you have plenty of control over how you view a situation and how long you allow something to stew. It is also a great way to model for the kids how to shake off a grumpy mood. There is no right way—just have fun and let go. You will eventually hit on your own version of pillow fighting. Do you know how hard it is to stay angry while dancing to disco? Donna Summer would tell you it is nearly impossible.

Chores—Part I

There was a time not so long ago when parents deliberately had huge families largely to ensure tons of help with farming and their households. Wow, how our collective societal mindset has shifted. I say bring back some of that work ethic and get the kids involved.

Chores are good for kids, teaching them responsibility, persistence, time management, and how to overcome resistance. As much as possible, take some of the duties off your list and delegate age-appropriate tasks to your children. As you do, remember that children often need to be patiently taught how to do what you now take for granted.

In *Secrets of Discipline*, educator and behavior specialist Ronald Morrish advises the following steps when teaching a child, regardless of age: start small, stay close, insist, and follow through. Although there is an up-front time investment as you instruct your child, it will save you time in the long run. It is also an opportunity to connect with your child while you work alongside him, especially during the learning phase.

Fortunately, my daughter is mostly amenable to helping around the house and with her little brother. If a bit of whining commences upon my request for help, I am quick to remind her of little Laura Ingalls rising before dawn for the farm chores and the two-mile trek to school, followed by more chores, babysitting, homework, and dinner preparation. Just to drive the point home, I may reference the frosty discomfort of the outhouse in the dead of night in winter. She either capitulates because of the story itself or to escape from my irritating recounting of it. Either way, it essentially makes it more unpleasant for her to resist the chores than to actually complete them. Gotta do what you gotta do.

> Forget about teaching your child lessons unless you're in a state of love and can teach lovingly. Anger and punishment are never based in love. A teachable moment is always when both people are receptive and positive.
>
> *—Dr. Laura Markham*

The Chores—Part I Mindful Break: Let go of the need to have tasks done just as you would do them. If you fear the completion will not live up to your standards, it may be a great opportunity to practice the Good Enough Mindful Break (page 221). You may be an expert laundry folder, but your little one is just learning.

Every six months or so, step back and take a look at the chores for which your children are responsible. It is easy to get stuck in the same routines and forget that as our kids grow and mature, they are able to learn and take on more responsibility, lifting some of the burden from you. When they do help out, show appreciation and reinforce how it allows you more energy and time to spend on what really matters to you—time with them high among those priorities.

Hit the Floor

It's in those exact moments when it feels as if there's not a moment to spare—when I am returning work emails, attacking a mile-long to-do list, or need to be dressed and out the door for work shortly—when the little guy morphs into a whiny, clingy whirling dervish in need of my attention *now*. Although it feels nearly impossible to stop what I am doing and focus my full attention on him, that is paradoxically precisely what we both need in that very moment.

I have learned to recognize this dance, although it never ceases to be uncomfortable and challenging. It often goes something like this: I am in hyper-focus-get-'er-done mode, which admittedly comes with a certain pleasant buzz of productivity. When the little guy's crankiness shows up, my initial reaction is to hang on to my to-do list even tighter. *Not now, I am getting stuff done! Mommy's on a roll! No interruptions!* This is when he usually turns it up a notch and I am unable to ignore it. If I am mindful enough to pause and notice, I realize, *Oh, yes, I see what is needed in this moment. He needs some undivided mommy attention ASAP.*

If I am not on my mindful game, however, we may go a few more rounds of whining and resisting before the pattern becomes clear. Often all that is required is a brief bit of my undivided attention to set us back on track once again. Seems our little ones often innately recognize when Mom needs a little mindful break before we do. There are times we'd do best to heed their wise advice. They're going to get us to stop one way or another, so we might as well strive to be mindful of their cues and prevent an impending emotional crash (theirs or ours). If you do miss the signs and a meltdown ensues, see After the Meltdown (Yours) Mindful Break (page 200).

The Hit the Floor Mindful Break: In those moments when you are intent on completing the infinite list and the kiddos begin to drive you crazy with interruptions, firmly but gently pause and step back from the situation. Forgive yourself when this seems difficult, as it often is.

Observe it as best you can from an outsider's perspective. Examine what is needed in this moment. Perhaps it's getting down on the floor to play Legos; perhaps it's pulling your child into your lap for a short snuggle or simply dropping whatever it is you are doing to give your teen your full attention as she recounts a noteworthy part of her day. The key here is offering your 100 percent uninterrupted attention. It is often much harder than it sounds. Notice the inevitable tug to get back to work. Breathe and stay, just for a brief while. Most often, as you return to your tasks, you will do so with less frantic, more mindful awareness. You might even thank your child for the opportunity to come back to what really matters.

After-School Snack

Although I am loathe to admit it, when my daughter embarked on her first day of kindergarten nearly a decade ago, I had secret visions of myself, all June Cleaver–like, offering warm, freshly baked chocolate chip cookies and milk on her arrival home each day. Fleeting fantasies they were; I'm quite sure I managed it the first day (and perhaps a smattering of other days in the following nine years), but for the most part, Beaver Cleaver's mom I am not. Sorry, honey.

What is it, though, about good old Mrs. Cleaver that is so appealing? When we strip away the frilly apron and permanently saccharine smile, what we're left with, ultimately, is a feeling of warmth, presence, and predictability. And that is very appealing. The cookies don't hurt, either.

Just as in the Bus Stop Mindful Break (page 70), where sending our children off to school in the morning is a convenient occasion conducive to pausing, connecting, reflecting, and sending our love off with them, their return from school offers a similar opportunity. A shared after-school snack is a perfect lure to place your kids right where you want them—in the kitchen with you, your willing captive audience for a short while.

With little ones it is satisfyingly obvious what sort of day they experienced at school. Guileless elementary school-age children tend to wear their emotions on their sleeves because they are much less practiced at putting on a happy face. If there is exciting news to share, she will have difficulty restraining herself. Partaking in an after-school snack together is a perfect opportunity to share in her heartwarming excitement and joy when it is fresh and alive. Conversely, if your child has had an especially challenging day, she may be unable to contain the tears, the accompanying story spilling out of her mouth automatically. Knowing that Mom will be there with open arms and a willing ear is often enough to sustain a child through her difficult day.

Now that my daughter is old enough to walk home from the bus stop with her neighborhood friends, there is no longer a need for me to wait at the corner for the bus to arrive, watching her bound down the steps and into my arms as she once did those seemingly long years ago. In fact, there are now times when she enters the house after school and I am so engrossed in writing that I barely register her arrival. But inevitably I do. Occasionally, I must force myself to stop mid-thought so I can go to her, give her a hug, and check in. Two days per week I am not home to greet her, and two other days per week I head out the door to the office a few minutes after she arrives, therefore gathering my belongings and wrapping up work at home as she walks in. I make an effort to have these items completed before she returns so that I am able to offer her my undivided attention for those brief fifteen minutes. Clearly not June Cleaver, but with some flexibility, we make it work. We eat, we talk. Some days she has little to divulge; other days she can plainly use the time to unload and share.

Even knowing our children as well as we do, we may need to become proficient at reading their nonverbal cues—what they do not say but what may be read in their gait, facial expressions, attitudes, and energy levels. Older kids might instinctively head immediately to their bedrooms. Sharing a ritual after-school snack offers at least a brief opportunity to notice, assess, and connect.

Sometimes what our children really need is simply our presence as well as some silence; or perhaps some energizing music is in order. The after-school snack ritual is one they will learn to count on whether they are consciously aware of it or not. It can become a grounding, comforting, predictable part of their day or week.

The After-School Snack Mindful Break: Whenever possible, create a habit of sharing an after-school snack with your children. Create a space in your schedule for this sacred time to reconnect. Prepare a simple snack, healthy and nourishing when possible, decadent and tempting when necessary. Do whatever you need to do within reason to get your child to eat and hang out with you. If that means cookies and milk, so be it. Make it appealing. Perhaps a bit manipulative, it's nevertheless offered in the most loving of ways. Food can be a wonderful motivator, especially for teens.

Sharing an after-school snack can also be a perfect way to allow conversation to flow naturally. If your child is younger, conversation may not be an issue, although many younger kids start answering the "How was school today?" question with one-word answers remarkably early. If this is the case, ask more open-ended questions such as "Tell me something that surprised you today. Who did you sit with at lunch? Tell me something that felt difficult today." As best you can, let the conversation and questions flow freely, so as not to bombard your child with an ostensible inquisition. Nothing will make him flee from the room more quickly than that.

Remind yourself that we cannot force conversation but merely create the conditions for it. As our kids grow older, naturally flowing candid conversation often becomes increasingly challenging and rare. Especially with teenagers, whenever possible we need to be open to listening on their timetables, not ours. By creating this after-school ritual, your children will come to expect and know deeply that you are there, in both body and true presence, if and when they need to talk.

Much like my workweek, if your family schedule does not lend itself to daily after-school snacks, try to carve out at least one day a week for this time to connect. You may need to get creative to make it workable for your family.

Tara, a work-outside-the-home mom I know, practices this mindful break every Friday afternoon. Before preparing dinner, she puts out a simple spread of grapes, cheese, and crackers as her two children, one a tween and the other a teen, congregate around the kitchen island to chat. They check in easily with one another, noticeably decompressing as they settle into the weekend. The kids sometimes wander off to their respective bedrooms after ten minutes or so, but more often than not end up hanging out in the kitchen while Tara begins dinner. Tara tells me this simple, anticipated weekly routine has opened up many an insightful conversation she might have otherwise missed. "My kids usually see me bustling around after work, but they know this is a time when everything stops and we are there for each other 100 percent. They know they have my full attention and I have theirs." No apron or freshly baked cookies required.

Homework

Homework. What is your immediate knee-jerk reaction to that word? Is it one of disgust and horror, accompanied by an acute sense of panic and shortness of breath? Maybe you react with calm impartiality, with neither positive nor negative connotation. Perhaps you experience the warm fuzzies, a sense of excitement and anticipation for shared pleasant memories with your child. Remarkably, homework can instantly precipitate either of these wildly varied reactions in moms everywhere, hinging often upon which of their children comes to mind and which stage of parenting they are in currently.

Depending on a whole host of factors, such as your children's unique personalities, ages, levels of motivation, and self-sufficiency, as well as how longstanding the homework habit and associated feelings about it are, homework may be one of your largest, most formidable challenges: one that is yet to be confronted, one that produces not a blink of an eye. If you find yourself squarely in the camp of dread, this mindful break may be one you utilize daily.

As with most things parenting, the attitude we moms bring to a situation, especially if it's historically fraught with angst, can set the tone for the interaction. Having said this, attitude, of course, is ultimately up to your child. Our demeanor and presence matters and can either hinder or help, but only up to a point. After all, each child is wildly different in innate personality, over which we have only so much control.

> Raising kids is part joy and part guerilla warfare.
>
> —*Ed Asner*

Perhaps, however, homework is not your current mothering challenge or is a neutral, or even a pleasant, daily occurrence in your home. If this is the case, count yourself lucky. Enjoy it while it lasts. Not to burst your homework-loving bubble, but eventually even the most studious children encounter some form of frustration or adversity in their academic careers. So, if and when it does arise and you find yourself in uncharted homework waters, you will have this mindful break to guide you.

The Homework Mindful Break: It's vital to first bring awareness to ourselves. Your initial reaction to the thought of homework can guide you here. If you are already woefully aware of a good amount of angst, anxiety, reluctance, or fear because you've been doing this homework thing now for some time and can't *not* notice this unmistakable reaction, calming yourself before it commences each day may be your starting point.

For some of us, there is a more subtle sense of dread due to the unpredictable nature of how homework will play out on any given night. Perhaps it typically proceeds smoothly, with the occasional major meltdown arising seemingly out of nowhere, often due to certain projects or subjects. It's disconcerting to be caught completely off-guard because the unpredictability can keep us feeling slightly anxious without our awareness.

So, first we must notice what we are experiencing, calming ourselves if necessary. We may need to ask ourselves how best to approach the child because what works for one may have the opposite effect for another. This is most often a series of trial and error. Then we need to hand over the reins to our children, step aside, and let the outcomes play out as they may. When in doubt, be involved as little as possible but step in when necessary. It's painful to watch our children struggle, but it's vital that we don't rush in immediately. Teaching your child to calm herself with breathing, to step away for a few moments to stretch or listen to music can be extremely helpful. And if your child continues to struggle daily, perhaps outside help is warranted.

Involve your child in crafting healthy homework habits that work for her. Even if you are skeptical, allow her to test them out.

If her idea of a workable routine does not produce the desired results, you may need to impose some structure of your own. As best you can, involve her in the discussion and compromise with solutions whenever possible. As your children grow, it is helpful for you to periodically reevaluate your level of involvement, creating independence whenever possible.

Most importantly, be continually mindful and curious of your own subtle body sensations, emotions, and thoughts when homework time rolls around. Keep breathing, relaxing tight muscles, and offering yourself compassion if needed for this common parenting challenge.

Sports and Performing

We've all heard (or witnessed) the Little League horror stories of parents acting ungraciously, taking the game and their children's role in it way too seriously. No one wants to be that sideline soccer parent cliché living vicariously through her children, but, I must admit, I understand how such a parent might evolve.

Whether you have a budding athlete, musician, artist, or academic, if you've found yourself watching your child perform in any capacity, you would be untruthful if you said you did not experience any reaction whatsoever. Whether we attempt to appear nonchalant or disaffected, we care deeply about our children's performance. Perhaps it's not so much because it matters to us how they do but because it matters so much to us how they feel and how they are affected by how they do—not to mention that as our children grow older the competition and the future stakes often increase as well.

We know our children so well, and at times this can be a blessing and a curse. As we read their body language and their faces we feel for them, perhaps imagining what they might be experiencing as we observe them succeed or fall short. We feel nervous for them. We feel elated for them. We feel proud of them. But this is exactly when we need to exercise the most caution. It's easy to get carried away. Most of us exert enough control over ourselves that we don't end up acting like the soccer parent cliché, though we may experience many similar (and hopefully less intense) thoughts, body sensations, and emotions. Perhaps your children have been performing for so long that it seems as if it's something you barely give a second thought to, but my guess is that in reality you experience some of these reactions as well.

> Meditation is not about fixing something that is broken. It's about discovering that nothing is broken.
>
> —*Jon Kabat-Zinn*

We are also fully aware of how so very brave it is of our children to try. When they are performing in any capacity, they are vulnerable—to criticism and evaluation by themselves, us, and others. And so, for us moms there are at least two layers to this situation. There is not only the performance itself, but also the critique by either well-meaning coaches or teachers and other parents, who often are the most harsh. It's difficult enough to sit and watch your child, sensing his nervousness and observing his concentration, without overhearing another parent comment on or, God forbid, yell at your child from the sidelines.

I have noticed the following reactions in myself—holding my breath, tightening my stomach, raising my shoulders, clenching my jaw, my heart rate increasing, and breathing more shallowly—all in anticipation of a performance. Sometimes these sensations have been most noticeable after the fact. After the performance, I realize how tightly I had been tensing my muscles, and after I take that first deep breath I recognize how shallowly I had been breathing. Of course, it's not always so unpleasant, and I have thoroughly enjoyed watching my children perform as well. I have felt my heart swell with pride, a huge grin on my face, tears in my eyes, and warmth in my chest filled with plenty of relaxed, deep breaths.

Even though we may know intellectually that mistakes or failures are actually healthy life lessons for our children, we cannot help but pray that it does not happen right now. Not this time—if she needs to fail, could we just make it next time? This time feels too painful. For us. If you have a child, you cannot help but feel some anxiety, tension, or nervousness when she is performing or evaluated in some way. It's just basic human nature. So how do we manage it?

Even if we keep our cool, our kids know us as well as we know them. They can easily sense our anxiety and tension. So rather than expend our precious energy attempting to hide it from them, use this mindful break to help calm yourself. The more awareness we have of our own thoughts, emotions, and body sensations, the less reactive and the more mindful of our responses we can be.

The Sports and Performing Mindful Break: As you watch your child perform, bring awareness to your breath. Often we hold our breath or breathe shallowly when feeling anxious or excited. Bring your attention to the three points on the Triangle of Awareness (page 31): What are your body sensations? Are your shoulders raised? Is your face tightened into a grimace? Where do you feel tension in the body? Can you relax those muscles? If you are breathing shallowly, take a few deep inhales and exhales.

What is the content of your thoughts? Are you critiquing your child? Are you imagining what he is thinking? Notice your thoughts and, as best you can, bring your attention back to the performance in front of you. Can you attempt to observe from a more objective position? Can you be curious and open to however it plays out? What emotions are present—Pride? Fear? Anticipation? Frustration?

When you are aware of your internal state, remind yourself that whatever develops, these are valuable life lessons and some struggle is healthy and instructive. Step back and gain perspective. You may also find it helpful to remember that even though it feels important at this very moment, it won't matter a year from now. (And if it truly will matter a year from now, go back to those breaths, my friend. It may matter, but probably not as much as it seems right now.) As many of us remind our children, it's not the end of the world. In fact, it's just the beginning of the rest of their lives.

STOP the Teen 'Tude

Before you had kids, what sort of mother did you imagine you would be? Calm? Loving? Steady? Fun? In control? Sure, we can be all of these at certain times. What surprised me the most, though, about becoming a mom was my inability to consistently embody these qualities while parenting the little creatures I love more than anything in the world. Such a paradox. Granted, I was not so naive as to think our days would look as saccharine as Julie Andrews joyfully singing, "The hills are alive with the sound of music." I am, however, repeatedly taken aback by my capacity when seriously provoked to feel like I've morphed into crazy-eyed Jack Nicholson in *The Shining*. (I'm sure it doesn't look as bad as it feels. *Right, honey? Wait, don't answer that.*) And it has only gotten more interesting as my little girl grows into the teen years.

This parenting thing is hard while living in the real world with real stresses, real responsibilities, and real personalities. And the teenage years bring with them a new set of challenges—challenges such as teen attitude, otherwise known as *the 'tude*.

My loving, sweet daughter has not long ago embarked upon adolescence. I can just hear all of you moms of older teens thinking something akin to, *She has no idea what is coming her way.* I know it, I believe you, and let me just say that there are times when denial is a beautiful thing. So it comes as a repeated surprise when my adoring daughter barks back at an innocent question with a mix of attitude, disgust, and dramatic eye roll. This is the moment when I fantasize about operating a remote control connected to a very subtle (I'm not a monster, after all) Taser gun, offering just enough of a shock to return her eyeballs to their rightful place and her countenance back to that of sweet, adoring daughter.

Children will teach you about yourself. They'll teach you that you are capable of deep compassion and also that you are definitely not the nice, calm, competent, clear-thinking, highly evolved person you fancied yourself to be before you became a mother.

—Harriet Lerner

Before you call the authorities, I did say *fantasize,* and it is very short lived, I assure you. I am not proud of this reaction, but humor does soften it by putting a little distance between me and the situation. What also keeps me from completely losing my cool is to pull out a STOP Mindful Break:

Stop. Take a breath. Observe. Proceed.

The STOP Mindful Break is not so much about ridding ourselves of the universal teen 'tude (although I wouldn't mind that) as it is about staying in control of ourselves when faced with it. Rarely does it go well if we are caught in our own emotional storm and, therefore, not thinking clearly. How much teenage sass we tolerate and what limits we set are up to each of us. But first we need to regulate ourselves before we can manage a potentially heated situation.

If I can catch myself when that teenage 'tude shows up, I can stop, take a few deep breaths, and check in with my body sensations. I am then better able to gather myself and provide her, in as calm a voice as I can muster, a warning to check her tone. Whatever comes next depends on a whole host of factors, but in the meantime I have regained some clarity and can proceed accordingly, all Taser and *Shining* scenarios (largely) vanished from my mind.

The STOP Mindful Break: When your teen offers up a 'tude, see if you can stay in control of yours. First, stop right where you are, whatever you are doing. Take a few deep breaths. Notice what is happening in your body. Is your jaw tight? Has your heart rate speeded up? Your breath quickened? Which muscles have tightened with anger? Most likely your thoughts

will persistently try to persuade you to fix the problem *now*. But first things first. The STOP Mindful Break will help you calm down enough to find the best solution, whether immediate or after given some time and thought. If needed (and it is often needed), repeat the first three steps until you feel calm enough to proceed. Stop. Take a breath. Observe. Proceed. Good luck (to us both). May the STOP Mindful Break help us remain just a little bit closer to that loving mommy version of ourselves we once imagined.

Dinner

In her wise TedTalk, Jennifer Senior, author of *All Joy and No Fun: The Paradox of Modern Parenthood,* shares this poignant quote by happiness researcher Matthew Killingsworth, PhD: "Interacting with friends is better than interacting with your spouse, which is better than interacting with other relatives, which is better than interacting with acquaintances, which is better than interacting with parents, which is better than interacting with our children. Who are on par with strangers."

Yowza. That is quite a statement. Granted, this is a generalized research finding that may or may not resonate with you. If I am being honest with myself, though, there are certainly instances when I can easily relate to this sentiment—one of them being dinner with little ones. And if this quote rings at all true for you, nightly dinners with those little heathens "on par with strangers" could be the cause of some serious indigestion. Short of popping a nightly antacid, what can we do about it? Fortunately, there are a few simple habits we can establish to minimize the chance of daily heartburn.

First, weekly meal planning is key. If this is not part of your routine, I encourage you to try it for a few weeks and notice the difference. Dinner prep, including what to cook while ensuring we have the ingredients on hand, is blissfully one less thing to occupy our busy minds and long to-do lists if we simply plan ahead. Because my husband is the primary cook, we sit together for a few minutes over coffee each Sunday to craft the upcoming week's menus. There is a dramatic disparity between the weeks when we have planned versus when we merely wing it. Without a prepared menu, we are not only scrambling at the last minute to conjure up a meal, but also making unnecessarily frantic trips to the grocery store to grab needed items, not to mention eating takeout more frequently, which is costly as well as unhealthy.

Second, I recommend setting up the conditions as best as possible for a pleasant, leisurely family dinner, then judiciously letting go of expectations. Now, depending on your style of parenting, dinner expectations can look like anything from a formal affair to a completely chaotic free-for-all. When my teenager was a wee one, our expectations landed somewhere in the middle. We taught her to eat patiently with us for a short while with some level of decorum. With my son my standards have relaxed even further, in part due to differing levels of energy and attention spans and in part due to having them ten years apart. Lucky for my son.

For, after a decade, I have witnessed that just because my daughter at age two did not sit at the dinner table longer than six minutes, it did not portend barbaric dinner behavior as a teen.

She is now clearly capable of a pleasant, civilized dinner, no harm done. And so, keeping this in mind, we allow our little guy to leave the table and run a few laps around the living room before he returns for a few more bites. I don't expect he will be doing this at age fourteen. At least, I hope not.

So, fully aware that our little guy at age four is guaranteed to remain seated for only the first three fleeting minutes of dinner, we often begin our meal by checking in with one another. If conversation does not flow easily, we might take turns sharing our highs and lows from the day. Even our preschooler is a willing participant. Soon up and moving again, the little guy engages sporadically in our conversation while allowing my husband, my daughter, and me the opportunity to talk more at length.

Fortunately, this controlled dinner chaos mellows over time. As kids grow and mature, they are naturally more apt to linger over lengthier exchanges. Now that my daughter is a teenager, I anticipate and relish insightful, engaging conversations with her and my husband at the dinner table. I love to hear about her full day, her thoughtful opinions, and whatever varied interests have captured her attention at the moment. What a difference a decade can make.

The Dinner Mindful Break: As best you can, set up the conditions for a mindful family dinner. Plan weekly menus to avoid the stressful, last-minute decision making. Depending on the age of your children and your concept of what is reasonable, perhaps lay down a few simple ground rules, such as how long each child is expected to remain at the table and ensuring that each family member has an opportunity to share (largely) uninterrupted.

You may want to light a candle and take a collective deep breath, pausing to offer a prayer, a few seconds of silence, or gratitude. You might teach your family members how to take one mindful bite of food, noticing keenly with their senses of sight, smell, and taste. With a gentle touch, remind yourself and your family to pause every so often, take a deep breath, and slow down, maintaining mindful attention to the food itself. It can also be helpful to enjoy the last bite with full awareness as well because it serves as a reminder throughout dinner that the last bite is yet to come, keeping us on our mindful toes.

If you'd like, go around the table sharing highs and lows from the day, offering each family member full attention. Most importantly, surrender any unrealistic expectations for a perfect family dining experience. Perfect doesn't exist, and forcing it will only backfire. If you are currently in the midst of wee-one-eating-bedlam, take solace in the fact that dinner will not look like pandemonium forever. In the meantime, there is always the trusty Wine Mindful Break (pages 233–34). Bon appétit.

Sibling Strife

Whatever the span in age of your children, there are certain advantages and disadvantages. The downsides to our family's ten-year sibling age gap are in creating family activities appropriate for both children, the shock to my system of a completely distinct second wave of diapers and sleep deprivation, and the logistics of always having children at two separate schools with different locations, start times, and end times.

Conversely, having my kids a decade apart also affords me countless benefits. I can easily enlist a (mostly) willing babysitter just down the hall, I've procured a bit of hard-earned mommy wisdom over the last ten years, and I regularly witness just how swiftly time flies as a dependable reminder to stop and smell the proverbial roses.

One might imagine another advantage of such a significant age difference: the absence of typical sibling strife between the two. In this case one would be *wrong, wrong, wrong*. Despite the fact that my fourteen-year-old is reasonably mature and self-controlled for her age, often when my children come within spitting distance of each other they not-so-magically mutate from fourteen and four into a pair of bickering toddlers. My son growls menacingly at his sister when she smothers him with hugs. She responds with a mature, "Fine! I'm not going to play with you!" as they commence swatting at the air and each other as if besieged by a swarm of killer bees, hands and arms flailing wildly. And then, of course, comes the universally heard sibling cry: "He started it!" *Sigh.*

Whenever possible, I walk (or run) away and allow them to negotiate the momentary crisis on their own. So far no one has been seriously maimed. Because what I have come to realize is that, just as quickly as they morph into bickering barbarians when I am around, when it is just the two of them alone they just as instantly become enamored with each other, sharing and laughing and playing and snuggling. Which means that while my husband and I are gratefully secure in knowing we can enjoy a date night out with little worry of what is happening at home, it takes about six seconds upon return before those sibling strife-filled beasts are back. Allowing them to work it out on their own, therefore, is something I know they are both capable of and is healthy for them (and me).

> Mindfulness gives you time. Time gives you choices. Choices, skillfully made, lead to freedom. You don't have to be swept away by your feeling. You can respond with wisdom and kindness rather than habit and reactivity.
>
> *—Bhante Henepola Gunaratana*

When I am caught captive and unable to walk away, however, such as while driving with them both squabbling in the car, more serious coping-skill reinforcement needs to be called in. What I have learned to do (after taking a few *deep* breaths) is imagine I am safely surrounded by a sibling-discord-proof bubble. My transparent bubble allows me to keep an eye on things should they get out of hand while blocking out all the unpleasant, frustrated little voices. This is not *always* effective, of course, and certainly there are times I am required by necessity to pop my blissful bubble and intervene, but when at all possible, into my bubble I go. Minimally, it provides me something on which to focus other than the irritating arguing. Ideally, I find a bit of peace in my delightful imaginary bubble. Inside it is silent save for the (also imaginary) birds chirping sweetly. Feigning temporary deafness toward my children, my face softens into a relaxed smile. More than likely it is a sort of semi-sound-permeable bubble because I am just not *that good*. I breathe, I imagine, I am yanked back into reality, I breathe again, I imagine . . . and on it goes.

Lest I have painted a most unpleasant picture of my beautiful children, thankfully their fighting is intermittent and inconsistent; they just as easily offer loving words and gestures to each other regularly. When that awful bickering arises, though, it is a stretch to recall the love-fest that was in full force not three minutes prior. If you have more than one child, I know you certainly can relate. This mindful break is for you.

The Sibling Strife Mindful Break: First, take a few deep breaths so as to regain some control over yourself and your automatic reactions. If your children are younger and the situation is especially heated, you may need to intercede to ensure a safe environment. Whenever possible, breathe first. Just as we moms benefit from a time-out in order to calm down and regroup, so do our kids. Time-outs are best thought of as an opportunity to de-escalate rather than as punishment. When we approach conflict with this kind, yet firm, attitude, our children learn that a mandatory time-out is not punitive but for the greater good of all involved. If the conflict does not seem to portend grave bodily harm, take those deep breaths and slowly envelop yourself in that lovely imaginary bubble where serenity rules. Bring awareness to your body, relaxing tight muscles in the shoulders, belly, and face. With a light-hearted attitude, be as creative as you'd like with the contents of your bubble. It is about refocusing and reframing the situation that matters most. If it is one of those times when your bubble simply isn't enough, it may be helpful to enlist some of the other mindful breaks, such as Turn Your Head (page 167) or This, Too, Is Passing (page 126), because it is passing; it always does. I promise.

This, Too, Is Passing

There is nothing quite so painful as seeing our children in distress and knowing there is very little we can do to take away their pain. Whether physical or emotional, the strong urge to take it on ourselves is universal. Feeling helpless is an intense emotion and, like all intense emotions, can cause us to act out in ways both unhelpful and regrettable.

My babies both suffered from acid reflux for a number of weeks. In the big scheme of things, I recognize this is a comparatively minor inconvenience and, believe me, I continue to count my blessings. Yet in the midst of day after day, night after night of inconsolable crying (theirs and eventually mine), the feeling of helplessness only increased in its magnitude. There were some nights that stretched on inconceivably, tortuously long, when I paced the floor for hours, desperate for the glimmer of sunrise so I could feel like a part of the human race once more (or at least could hand the baby off to my husband or call someone without waking her from a dead sleep).

> When you come to the end of your rope, tie a knot and hang on.
>
> —*Franklin D. Roosevelt*

Fast-forward three years. I am driving in the car, my little guy riding in the back, strapped into his car seat, beside himself with nervousness. Tears are pouring out from under those lush, dark eyelashes, and his face has grown blotchy from the sobbing. It's his first day attending the nearby preschool I have enrolled him in three mornings a week, and he is begging me not to go. In his heartbreakingly sweet three-year-old mind, he is conjuring up all sorts of rationalizations as to why he should not go, including the assertion that he is fine to stay home alone when I tell him I need to go to work (which, by the way, is a flat-out lie I resorted to in desperation—I am sending him because I believe strongly he will love it once he acclimates—but I obviously can't tell him *that*).

Fortunately, the car ride to preschool is only five and a half minutes (that half minute counts when it feels as if someone is tearing your heart out, trust me), and after the first week the tears and begging thankfully have ceased. In fact, on the first morning before school of the second week, my little guy looks at me and says, "Do you think I should cry today before school?" I tell him I don't think it's necessary. And that is that.

As for the reflux, I obviously managed to survive that as well. As everything does, this stage mercifully passed and now induces only the slightest facial twitch when remembered. What helped me cope in the midst of both of our suffering was grounding myself in the awareness of my breath and repeating this mantra over and over: *This, too, is passing. This, too, is passing.* If you saw me, you might have mistaken me for a woman who had lost her mind. But, actually, it was just the opposite. I was clinging to my sanity with the help of a simple mindful phrase: *This, too, is passing.*

The This, Too, Is Passing Mindful Break: Whether it's consoling a newborn or a heartbroken teenager, it's helpful to first take a few deep breaths and notice what is present in our body sensations so we can be more present for our children. Is there a panicky, hollow feeling in the belly, a squeezing pressure in the chest? Has the pace of breath quickened slightly?

Offer yourself some kindness and compassion for the appearance of the uncomfortable sensations and associated emotions of helplessness and sadness. Use the awareness of the breath as a home base to rest your attention when it begins to feel overwhelmed with the emotions of the situation. Whenever that feeling of helplessness shows up (and it will, again and again in this roller-coaster marathon of parenting), hang on to the awareness of each inhale and exhale and the knowledge that *this, too, is passing, this, too, is passing.* Because it always does, eventually, inevitably leaving us with a much greater appreciation for those once neutral-, now blissful-feeling times when we can coast for a while.

Look into Their Eyes

Sometimes the simplest moments in life are also the most profound—the sorts of moments that cause us to sit up straight and take notice, lifting the veil of mindlessness from our eyes. As is true for many of us, several things simultaneously compete for my attention and time: three-year-old, thirteen-year-old, husband, family, work, chores, friends, exercise, volunteering, and so on. A champagne problem, indeed; I am grateful for it all, but I can nevertheless feel overwhelmed at times by the sheer volume of it.

This has been especially true since my little guy arrived because he requires so much of our energy. A funny, energetic boy full of joy, he easily draws us in, commanding the room with his engaging toddlerisms. My daughter adores him and, despite her first ten years of life as our family's only child, only on rare occasions complains about his existence. For better or worse, he is the squeaky wheel, the proverbial kid in the class whose hand shoots up when a question is asked. *Oooh, oooh! Pick me! Pick me!* Yes, my love, you have my attention . . . and my time.

One recent weekend afternoon I was slowed down with a cold. While my son was napping, my daughter and I sat outside on the patio and chatted. I was too exhausted for chores or tossing the ball, so we simply sat, our full attention on each other, uncharacteristically free of distraction. As we talked, I looked into her eyes, struck by the once-familiar brilliance of the green, blue, and gold kaleidoscope pattern found there. My breath caught in my throat. I was both amazed and horrified that I had forgotten their exquisiteness.

And in that moment I recognized just how unmindfully I had been communicating with her—not really seeing her, usually with partial attention, often in the middle of another mundane household task. I felt sad yet grateful for the realization that my lovable thirteen-year-old had taken a backseat to far too many insignificant preoccupations.

I had gradually fallen into a habit of placing her toward the bottom of my potentially endless list—certainly not in terms of importance or love, but rather in regard to when she would receive my full attention: after the diaper was changed, the dog was fed, the work emails returned. At the end of each long day, after the little guy was in bed and we finally had uninterrupted time together, little energy remained for my sweet, tolerant girl.

I don't want to get to the end of my life and find that I lived just the length of it. I want to have lived the width of it as well.

—Diane Ackerman

Just as the quiet, compliant student is often overlooked in the classroom, so had my little girl silently and inadvertently slipped under my mommy radar. So, with more than a hint of guilt and humility, I made a silent promise to both her and myself—I will do my best to look into those beloved eyes with more frequency and more awareness.

At times I still need to force myself to stop the doing in the midst of the list, to go to her and connect. Rather than give her half my attention while cleaning up the kitchen, I must remember to sit down, look into those beautiful eyes, and hear about all the magnificent, insightful goings-on behind them.

Just as it's easy to fall off course, it's also easy to adopt one simple, deliberate, mindful change to correct direction. For me it has made such a remarkable difference placing my daughter back in her rightful position at the top of my list, flying well within the parameters of my mommy radar. I fear what I might have missed. I am grateful for the opportunity to continually refocus my lens of attention.

The Look into Their Eyes Mindful Break: Each moment is an opportunity for us to refocus our lens of attention. My wish for us all is this: Stop what you are doing. Look into your child's eyes. Take a breath. Drink it in. This can become increasingly challenging as our kids grow and aren't literally in our direct line of vision constantly. Make a silent, loving promise to yourself to savor what really matters. See how one small mindful break can potentially transform an ordinary moment into one that feels remarkable.

The Live-In Zen Master

As parents we are continually teaching and guiding our children, but we often lose sight of what it is we can learn from them. In *Everyday Blessings: The Inner Work of Mindful Parenting,* Myla and Jon Kabat-Zinn refer to our kids as little live-in Zen masters. When we slow down long enough to notice and are open, we see that our children are full of sage observations, almost seemingly just waiting patiently for us to be receptive to their wisdom. They *live* mindfulness, after all.

From the newborn who leaves us no choice but to slow down the pace to a crawl, to the toddler pausing on his way out of the house to examine a bug, to the teen who decides that 10:30 PM is a great time to launch into an honest, important conversation—they are operating on their own mindful timetable, not ours. When at all possible, can we pause and inhabit their mindful time zone as well? This is not always realistic, of course, and we should not set ourselves up for unattainable expectations. Don't worry—often when we aren't paying attention, we eventually manage to receive the message loud and clear one way or another. Let me share a story.

> If we learn to open our hearts, anyone, including the people who drive us crazy, can be our teacher.
>
> —*Pema Chödrön*

My little guy's belly laugh should come with a warning, something like, CAUTION: MAY CAUSE SERIOUS BODILY HARM. MAY BE HIGHLY ADDICTIVE. The other day I woke up in pain, my neck and shoulders a hot mess of pinching, stabbing discomfort accompanying any sort of movement. I soon found myself at my chiropractor's office; she asked what I had been up to lately that might have been the cause. Chagrinned, I reluctantly shared how I might have been a little overzealous with my head-banging moves while dancing with my toddler. Don't judge, as my teenager would say.

You see, my husband is a talented songwriter who has recorded some very catchy, danceable tunes. Our son, who is his biggest fan, can't get enough of Daddy's music. As I started singing along and swinging my hair 360 degrees like a bad eighties backup dancer, my boy thought it was hilarious. He threw back his head of curls as laughter reverberated from deep in his belly. I was instantly hooked.

So, despite the fleeting voice of reason warning me that I may live to regret the outdated (both in music and body) moves, I very unmindfully persisted. We were having so much fun. He was bestowing the laugh with abandon. Like an addict desperate for another fix, I continued, carried away with the hope of another addictive belly laugh hit.

As I lay facedown on my chiropractor's table, I tentatively glanced over at my three-year-old live-in Zen master, who sat there listening with a half-grin on his wise little face as if to say, *What can I say? She gets carried away. I mean, can you blame her? Check out this adorable dimple and these lush, dark eyelashes.* Yes, he is well aware of the power he has over me. I am a total sucker for him. You would be, too, if you gave birth to him.

Mindfulness encourages us to find more balance in our busy lives by increasing the joy through play, fun, and laughter. The key here is balance. And so I was poignantly reminded that there is, indeed, such a thing as too much of a good thing; whether Ben & Jerry's, work, wine, or dancing, you can be sure if you aren't maintaining balance in your life, a lesson will eventually present itself for your learning pleasure. Just ask my little guy. Children are innately more mindful and tend to honor their body cues more readily. We adults are more conditioned to ignore our body signals, thereby injuring ourselves more easily (well that, and the fact that my forty-something-year-old joints aren't quite as well oiled as they once were).

When we regularly practice mindfulness, we tend to naturally maintain a sense of balance and moderation. It's when we are unaware or, in my case, choose to ignore what we know to be in our best interest that we veer off course. The beauty of mindfulness is that each moment is a new opportunity to begin again. From here on in, you can bet I will be moving and dancing with a bit more awareness.

Oh, but that belly laugh . . . This besotted mama is already searching for another way to get my next fix. My little guy is right; can you blame me? No one ever said mindfulness was perfection. In this case I'm not even going to try. Why fight it?

The Live-in Zen Master Mindful Break: When your child is calling for attention, pause, take a deep breath, and ask yourself, *What might I learn in this moment from my little Zen master?* (I know there will be times when the little—or big—Zen master seems more like a pain in the tush than a wisdom-filled guide. Perhaps that is exactly the time you might want to pay close attention.) Can you be open to receiving what lessons arise? Obviously this is not to say you leave all parenting in the hands of your kids. Horror of horrors. Rather, can you view motherhood as a journey you are on together, where you are willing to recognize when you have gotten off course or acknowledge an imperfection within yourself?

This may take a good dose of courage and self-forgiveness as well as the ability to own and apologize for our mistakes. On the other hand, it can also open avenues for beautiful shared moments as we occasionally pause and let our little wise ones take the lead, allowing them to remind us and share some of their fascination with what we often view as ordinary. My children have reminded me to stop doing and just listen, to pull myself out of my thoughts and notice the beautiful sunset or the way the light coming through the bedroom window casts a shadow that looks remarkably like a rhinoceros. I can only imagine what I miss when my teachers are not around to enlighten me.

May we be open to their lessons. May we allow them to bring out the best in us. May we, much like our children do naturally, live more in the present moment.

Prepping to Launch

We all want our kids to grow up to be happy, successful, well-adjusted adults. As a society, though, it seems we have gotten away from a healthy definition of what it means to be successful. The pressure for kids to succeed at everything from sports to academics to the arts is at an all-time high. Success is now equated with squeezing in as many activities as possible (because it looks good on the college application) while maintaining that above-4.0 GPA, while specializing in a sport or related art—all before becoming a legal adult. It causes me to break out into a recovering perfectionist sweat just thinking about it.

It's no wonder, then, that I hear tales of parents doing everything for their teens—science projects, laundry, packed lunches, even college application essays—because the perfectionistic expectations placed on our kids (by society, themselves, or us parents) are impossible to attain. Although it may originate from a loving place, we are not serving our children by completing for them what they can do on their own, even if that means it's done imperfectly or perhaps not done at all. If we are being honest with ourselves, we might recognize that our overdoing arises from an anxious, fearful place inside. *What if my child is not capable? What if he fails? What if she falls short? I'll help her out this one time.*

> Kids don't stay with you if you do it right. It's the one job where, the better you are, the more surely you won't be needed in the long run.
>
> *—Barbara Kingsolver*

I easily see how we might inadvertently find ourselves here—it's painful to see our kids fall—yet it's a dangerously slippery slope for moms to walk. First, despite our attempts to keep it hidden, our kids sense our anxiety and may internalize it, eventually doubting their own abilities. Second, when we jump in just this once to save them, we set up the likely expectation of it happening again. And it reinforces the message that we question their competence. Finally, we are not preparing them for the real world—for struggle, for failure, for independence, for resilience—because struggle builds resilience, one of the most valuable qualities we can foster in our children. The opposite of resilience—helplessness—is the belief that we are incapable of handling a situation and often goes hand-in-hand with anxiety.

It's a gift to teach our children how to believe in themselves, in their ability to figure it out and to tolerate whatever life throws their way. When we require them to step up to the plate, especially if we have rushed in to help quickly in the past, they will most likely resist. Change is uncomfortable for everyone. Expect the pushback and firmly but kindly hold your ground. Be consistent and trust that they are more capable than we realize. Give your children plenty of opportunities to make missteps while still under your care. Many times this means letting go and getting out of their way. That, my friends, is a large part of growing a successful adult. One of the most helpful guiding questions for us moms to keep in mind is, *Am I preparing her to launch?*

Their learning, of course, includes trial and error, success and failure. Without all of it, there is little growth. And so it's vital that we search inside ourselves and recognize when the pull to mother comes purely from our own needs, not theirs; when it comes from avoiding potential discomfort versus lending a helping hand out of love. There will, of course, be times we choose to do something for our child that he is perfectly capable of doing for himself. Every school day morning since kindergarten, for example, I have awakened before my daughter and prepared her tea and toasted her bagel before rousing her from sleep. In contrast, I have friends whose kids wake them with a good-bye on their way out the door. Wondering if I were doing my daughter a coddling disservice, I asked myself, *Am I preparing her to launch?* To answer that as honestly as possible, I examined this long-held habit using the Prepping to Launch Mindful Break litmus test, of which there are two parts.

The first part is assessing my own motivation. I am an early riser, already having meditated and caffeinated before she wakes up. Preparing her breakfast is something I choose to do out of love. The key here is *choose*. I do this willingly, not begrudgingly, not resentfully, not with a sense of martyrdom or anxiety.

The second part is assessing if this is something she is capable of completing independently. The answer, of course, is yes, she is certainly old enough to wake herself and slather some cream cheese on a bagel. On weekends, however, she often does prepare her breakfast and lunch, so I feel confident that she has mastered this skill. On both counts, then, this one passes the Prepping to Launch litmus test, and my teenage princess will continue to be served her tea and bagel before school.

There are circumstances in which I catch myself wanting to rescue when I see her struggling, but I manage to refrain. When she has not managed time well, for example, and is feeling pressure to study and complete chores at bedtime, I must hold myself back from lending a hand. Often, I first need to take a few breaths, walk away, and investigate: *Am I prepping her to launch?* When I have determined that stepping in is not the best choice for her in the long run, I might busy myself with some other task (the mom-equivalent of sitting on my hands and duct-taping my mouth shut). I know she needs to learn from that struggle, from that mismanagement of time, as difficult as it may be for me to watch. This is challenging enough when the stakes are low but a major feat of restraint when the stakes are high. As you practice this mindful break and watch your child stretch himself, it eventually fosters confidence in you both. Who couldn't use more of that?

The Prepping to Launch Mindful Break: Take those few deep breaths to gather yourself, calm your body, and help focus your thoughts. Keeping the question *Am I prepping him to launch?* in the forefront of our minds helps guide us. Then run the situation through the two-part litmus test.

First, check in with yourself. Are you feeling anxious? Scared? If so, how does this manifest in body sensations? Butterflies in the stomach? Pressure in the chest? Could your eagerness to protect be arising from your own fears, needs, or doubts? If the answer is yes, offer yourself some compassion for this difficult part of the mothering job that requires plenty of courage and blind faith. We need to learn to recognize and tolerate our own anxiety surrounding our kids' abilities and struggles so they can evolve.

Second, assess her capabilities. Deciding if our children are up to certain challenges is rarely a clear, easy decision, so we need to test the waters a bit. I think it's best to err on the side of confidence; we humans tend to rise to the challenge placed before us as long as it's clear someone believes in us. So if the answer is yes, or even a maybe, I encourage you to let go. Step out of the way. Remember, you will be there to catch her if she falls. But first, see if you can imagine her soaring. Happy launching.

CHAPTER 4

Connecting with Yourself During the Day

I am blessed with two healthy children, a daughter who is fourteen and a son who is four, as of this writing. Yes, they are ten years apart and, yes, it was a bit of culture shock returning to the world of diapers and sleep deprivation after several years. I began a daily meditation practice when my daughter was three. Meditation soon became as habitual as my morning shower, fortifying my life with an overall sense of calm and well-being, although it has not always been smooth sailing.

My little guy went through a bit of a rough ride in utero. A few weeks before my forty-first birthday, I was elated to discover that I was expecting. Although I was at advanced maternal age (which I lovingly referred to as geriatric pregnancy), I felt healthy and ready to begin this new chapter in our family's life. Two months into the pregnancy, a routine biopsy of a lump on my cheek turned up as basal cell carcinoma, the more treatable form of skin cancer. I was scared and anxious to hear that I would need to be put under in order to remove it. My most pressing concern was how it would affect the baby. In the week leading up to the procedure, I used my mindfulness practice to ground myself in the awareness of my breath when the worries began overtaking my mind.

After the relief of waking up after surgery to hear the strong heartbeat of the baby through the fetal heart monitor, my mindfulness practice helped me through the shock of seeing two dozen large, black stitches encircling the angry-looking incision on my left cheek. I cried. I felt the sadness in my body, the lump in my throat, and the sick feeling in the pit of my stomach all mixed with relief that the baby was OK. Mindfulness helped me acknowledge the feelings, give them their due, and then move forward, accepting what could not be undone.

Fast-forward two months. Following an afternoon preparing our garden for some fall planting, it became alarmingly clear as my pregnant body harshly rebelled and reacted that I had pulled out many small poison sumac plants. Admitted to the hospital for four days, I experienced a terrifying seizure-like reaction when IV medication was administered too quickly. The ability to calm myself with my breath and notice when the what-ifs were taking up residence in my mind helped to ease the discomfort. It did not eliminate the trials I faced, but it offered me a place to rest my attention for a short while.

My gardening efforts on hold, summer turned to fall and fall to winter when our long-awaited babe arrived. Thankfully, my little guy did not experience any adverse effects as a result of my pregnancy health issues. So here was this beautiful little baby boy—so wanted, so loved, and so not into sleeping for more than twenty minutes at a stretch. Combine this with breast-feeding difficulties including mastitis, our family worried sick about my mother-in-law suffering from terminal cancer, and a ten-year-old daughter yearning for some attention from her mom—postpartum depression soon became an unavoidable reality.

I vividly remember lying in my bed sobbing, wishing I could just disappear. I thought about my baby boy, my husband, my parents, and the devastating image of my daughter growing up without her mom. That was the closest I have ever come to feeling suicidal. I had no plan to end my life. I was too exhausted for that. I just wanted desperately to disappear. It was intense and scary.

Mindfulness did not prevent those powerful feelings, nor did it take away the emotional exhaustion and pain. But amid survival mode, I was able to remember something I knew well from practicing every day—given time everything changes, and this, too, would change. In fact, this, too, was changing. I would eventually be OK if I could just take it moment by moment. And that is exactly what I did until I was able to take it hour by hour, day by day, allowing the desperation to subside until I began to feel like myself again.

Jon Kabat-Zinn, founder of the world-renowned Mindfulness-Based Stress Reduction program, refers to this as "living the full catastrophe." We can develop the inner resources to tolerate and withstand whatever life brings our way, and that is a powerful antidote to anxiety, to the feeling that we need to have everything under control. A regular practice of mindfulness can help us by offering a home base, a familiar place of quiet, stillness, and peace in the midst of the storm.

This chapter provides mindful breaks that encourage you to consistently bring more self-care, peace, and fun to your days. You will learn ways to cope with life's challenges, cheer yourself on, and bring more mindful attention—and perhaps even some delight—to the mundane. So whether you are in need of a lifeline, some much needed TLC, or a mommy high five, you have come to the right place.

Wonder Woman

As my daughter embarks upon adolescence, I find myself once again thrown into the treacherous social world of teen girls. My bright, funny, insightful fourteen-year-old possesses staunch opinions and is not afraid to assert them. I assure you she did not inherit this from me. The truth is, I have really only found my voice in the past decade or so. And although I wasn't a complete doormat until that time, speaking up assertively was accomplished only occasionally and with a decent amount of discomfort. As a teen and young adult, I thought there was little worse than being called bossy or (gasp!) the other B word. I was going for *nice*. That is what I wanted to hear and usually did, at times to my own detriment. A born pleaser, assertiveness has been a hard-earned skill and one that in certain circumstances challenges me still.

Mothering from the sidelines (endeavoring to stay out of the helicopter), I vacillate between awe at my daughter's strength and angst that she may push it too far. I attempt to find balance between wanting to cheer her on for her chutzpah and advising her to just be quiet and let it go. I dare to hope that when faced with future peer pressure, my daughter will have built a solid arsenal of comfort in saying no and staying true to herself. Yes, I want her to be kind to others. Kindness is one of my most deeply held values. However, girls are expected to be *nice* (read *passive* and *quiet*), which is different than *kind*. What is often forgotten is kindness toward oneself and attending to one's own needs, especially for females in a society that still prioritizes and encourages niceness at the expense of leadership and assertiveness. Imagine if all of us females stopped worrying about *nice* and started channeling what I like to think of as our inner Wonder Woman. To me, Wonder Woman represents assertiveness, power (used only for good—she's going to kick your a#$ only if you deserve it), and self-confidence (I mean, you'd need to be seriously self-confident just to be seen in public in that getup).

> Life shrinks or expands in proportion to one's courage.
>
> —*Anaïs Nin*

Amy Cuddy, PhD, a social psychology researcher and associate professor at Harvard University, recently wrote a book entitled *Presence* in which she shares a fascinating study she conducted on body language. In the study, research participants were told to stand tall with their feet apart, hands on their hips, and heads held high for two minutes. (Imagine Wonder Woman standing to powerfully face her enemy.) Saliva samples were taken from participants before and after the two minutes of "power posing."

Amazingly, cortisol levels (the stress hormone) in the participants' saliva decreased while their testosterone levels (responsible for confidence and assertiveness) rose. This finding indicates that not only does our body language send a message to others about how we perceive ourselves, it actually alters our hormonal makeup.

> Don't shrink yourself to make others feel more comfortable
>
> *—Bria Simpson*

Since sharing this potentially life-changing information in a TedTalk a few years ago, Dr. Cuddy has heard from hundreds of people who now use it, revealing countless anecdotes of how it has changed their lives for the better. Those two minutes may not instantly transform you into Wonder Woman, but they do generate small shifts in your hormonal makeup. Rather than "fake it until you make it," Cuddy encourages us to "fake it until you become it"—assertive, powerful, and self-confident just like Wonder Woman—with, thankfully, no need for the unforgiving bodysuit.

The Wonder Woman Mindful Break: Spend two minutes per day in Wonder Woman pose. You can do this before or after brushing your teeth, while standing on the sidelines of your child's soccer game, or as an opportunity to check in with your triangle of awareness (body sensations, thoughts, and emotions). Throughout the day, bring your attention to your posture. Are you shrinking and making yourself smaller? Can you subtly take up a bit more space? Can you sit or stand tall, exuding confidence? Remember, we will not feel confident all the time, but we can fake it until we become it. Our posture matters. Our body language is a powerful form of communication. Go ahead and channel your inner Wonder Woman in the midst of your day. Who knows what you may conquer while exerting your benevolent power.

Driving

A few years back, I was on my way to a morning gathering of mindfulness teachers. Each month we met at someone's home to meditate, discuss relevant research, and learn new methods of instruction. This morning I was delighted to be driving the carpool with my two friends and fellow teachers for the hour-long trip. Absorbed in catching up with one another, I was inadvertently lulled into autopilot mode as we made our way down the interstate. Some miles later we were swiftly snapped out of our engrossing conversation as we realized we had just passed our turnpike exit. Imagine our chagrin as we arrived late for our mindfulness group, admitting with a chuckle how we had been quite *unmindful* en route to our monthly mindfulness meeting.

Even with the cell phone tucked away and no other immediate distractions, we all shift into autopilot at times, particularly when driving along a familiar route. Our minds, much like toddlers bouncing from one activity to the next, often become bored and look for something new and novel to engage them. The reasons are both numerous and obvious as to why we might want to be more mindful on the road—it is safer, it feels calmer, and it is one more opportunity to build that mama mindfulness muscle.

The Driving Mindful Break: As you drive, make the effort to check in with your body every few minutes or every few miles. Red traffic lights or waiting in traffic are also perfect reminders to practice mindful driving. Is your posture straight, yet relaxed? Can you drop your shoulders? Are your hands tightly gripping the wheel? Have your attention and thoughts wandered off the road? If so, steer them back to the present moment. What is the feel of your pace? Are you rushing and tense or relaxed and at ease? Are you running late? If so, take a deep breath, take a wider perspective, and assess if being late is really as crucial as it may feel. It rarely is. You're on your way, so why not enjoy the ride?

Nap Time

We have all heard the advice to new moms: Sleep when the baby sleeps. It's said with great intention, but I see a major flaw in this piece of wisdom. After all, whose newborn sleeps longer than thirty minutes at a stretch? If yours did, you are a rare and fortunate breed. I remember feeling like the starting gun was fired when the little guy would doze off and I (*Quick! Hurry up!*) ran to use the bathroom, gobbled up some food, and laid my weary head down, conscious of the seconds ticking away. It would take a mere sixty seconds for me to fall into a blissful dreamland and another five minutes for the babe to wake up fully rested and ready to party. It seemed like a cruel joke. I felt tortured by sleep deprivation and looked on in awe at other new moms who didn't seem to be completely decimated by it.

Desperate, I hung on to the thought that there would come a time when he would take what one might refer to as a proper nap (also knowing that the first time this happened I would be checking on a strangely quiet child—*is he OK?*), and until then, I needed to grab sleep whenever and however I could.

Shonda Rhimes, creator of *Grey's Anatomy*, recently wrote a funny and inspirational book called *Year of Yes*. Reading a chapter on motherhood, I learned that not only do we share a rare first name, but Ms. Rhimes and I share an agonizing relationship with sleep deprivation as well. She recounts how, eight weeks after her daughter was born, she was "sobbing from exhaustion so total that I felt sure I could SEE the air moving in blue waves around the room." *Yes, she gets me*, I thought. There was something perversely reassuring in reading this. It is not just me. She also writes, "Twelve years later the memories of those nights, of the sleep deprivation, still make me rock back and forth a little bit. You want to torture someone? Hand them an adorable baby they love who doesn't sleep."

I am telling you this not so you can resume rocking back and forth in remembrance like dear Shonda or run horrified for the hills to the land of the childless forever. No, no. I tell you this because we do not talk about it nearly enough, mostly because there is shame attached to feeling like we can't handle it, believing that everyone else manages so there must be something wrong with me if I am exhausted and drowning. But, as you see here, it is not just you, and sleep is a crucial part of our well-being as moms.

When sleep is once again reasonably under your control, you may find yourself falling into the culturally revered I'll-sleep-when-I'm-dead camp. Purposeful sleep deprivation—getting by on four or five hours a night—is not a badge of honor. So, whatever stage of mothering and sleep deprivation you are currently in, I encourage you to get more sleep. We need adequate sleep for both our physical and mental health. Most of us don't get enough, and research now indicates that chronic sleep deprivation causes real harm. Protect your sleep when possible and be an advocate for a solid seven to nine hours. The quantity and quality of our sleep are not always under our control, but whenever possible, place it high on your list of priorities.

Because my bedtime and wake times are not always completely in my hands, I have become the master of power naps and, fortunately, my work schedule allows it a few times per week. I think naps are brilliant and everyone should try them. I now have it down to a science. I set my phone alarm for precisely thirty-five minutes—five minutes to allow my mind to slow down and drift off to sleep, and thirty to doze blissfully. It is now at the point where, more often than not, I awaken a few moments before the alarm rings, refreshed and ready to proceed with my day. If I allow myself to sleep past that magic thirty minutes, I wake up groggy and grumpy (sounds like a few of the Seven Dwarfs); trust me, neither my family nor I want to deal with me when I am in this state, despite how hard I try to fake it. I can and do occasionally power through the tiredness, sometimes with the aid of caffeine, sometimes with sheer will, and sometimes with no other choice. None of these options comes close to my half-hour power nap, a much more mindful and kind way to recharge my mama batteries.

The Nap Time Mindful Break: If your children are younger and have an established nap time, or if they are old enough to entertain themselves without parental supervision, designate some nap time for your self-care.

If your kids no longer nap, are home with you, and are not old enough to entertain themselves, reinstate nap time in the form of quiet time. Teach them that for a short period of time, Mommy will be resting without interruption. Perhaps you let them know they need to remain in their bedrooms playing quietly or reading. They can learn—be firm and persistent. This quiet time is good for everyone. Whether or not they recognize it, we all need some time to decompress in silence. In our busy, stimulating society, it is a skill that needs to be taught and nurtured.

Establish this mindful break now so that when your kids are older they may return to the quiet voluntarily to recharge themselves. Perhaps you spend the time meditating, reading, or just staring off into space. The bottom line is to take a small portion of time for self-care and rest so you can be the best form of yourself for you and your family.

However you set up this mindful break for yourself, protect it. When that lovely time rolls around each day, first assess what is needed. How is your physical energy level? Are you awake, or is your energy flagging? How is your emotional state—drained or calm? The answer may be obvious or more subtle. If in doubt err on the side of rest. Experiment with the length of time you nap. Like me, there may be some sweet spot that offers you the ideal amount of energy. Too little and it's not enough and too much and you may end up feeling like one of the cantankerous Seven Dwarfs.

Waiting

As busy moms, we often feel as if there is nary a moment to spare. Waiting in line at the grocery store, in the after-school pickup line, or for that slow-as-molasses toddler to make his way from the bathroom to the bedroom can feel excruciatingly long. Impatience can build progressively as we mentally tick off all that could be accomplished with this time. Rather than feed the frustration, however, we can use waiting time as a built-in reminder to pause for a short mindful break. Over time, we often begin to invite—and even look forward to—those opportunities to further our awareness and presence.

> One thing that meditation shows us is that the sense of peace already exists within us. We all have a deep desire for it even if it is often hidden, masked, thwarted.
>
> —*The Dalai Lama*

The Waiting Mindful Break: While waiting, the urge to pick up the phone, text, or surf the Web may feel like a strong magnetic force. Before you succumb, just notice how you're feeling. Take a few deep breaths. If you are accustomed to filling up every spare moment with activity (such as compulsive phone checking), it can feel downright uncomfortable. Much like you would with your child, kindly but firmly encourage yourself to stay put. Beginning with your feet, scan up your body, noticing sensations in each body part. Release those muscles that are tense and can be loosened. Relax your belly. Drop your shoulders. Soften those small muscles around the mouth and eyes. Be aware of each inhale and each exhale. Each time you feel the pull to do something, challenge yourself to continue just to be mindful and notice your thoughts and feelings. The more you practice the Waiting Mindful Break, the more you will notice your increased ability to be still, less distracted, patient, and calm.

Chores—Part II

Cleaning the house has always been one of my least favorite responsibilities. I have long since given up hoping I would one day wake up and be more like one of my two friends—one actually loves cleaning just for the sake of cleaning, and the other cleans to relieve stress. Nope, not me. And, like many moms I know, my standards of cleanliness have been wildly altered since having children. There has been more than a little giving in and giving up. This is not to say that my house would be considered an official environmental hazard, just that we could feasibly count a few of those dust bunnies as honorary members of our family.

Every so often the day comes when I look around and realize some deep cleaning can't be put off any longer. Yesterday was one of those days. Feeling particularly reluctant about the impending cleaning session, I decided to bring some mindfulness to the experience. Rather than hang on to my resistance to the distasteful process itself, I chose to focus on the sensations of water, cloth, and vacuum. Whenever I noticed my mind drifting toward the familiar thoughts of loathing, I escorted it firmly, but kindly, back to simply noticing sensations one moment at a time.

I'd love to report that my little experiment inspired some blissful sense of oneness with my cleaning products, but let's not get carried away. Practicing some mindful cleaning did, however, take much of the distasteful bite out of the tasks, and I actually found myself slightly enjoying the process. Is it wrong that I kind of liked watching the little family of dust bunnies being sucked up by the vacuum? Who couldn't use a little more of that—the overall enjoyment, not the twisted dust bunny part, that is. Although I am not suggesting you need to find chores wildly entertaining, bringing mindfulness to the task at hand and accepting whatever it is we are engaged in—even the most unpleasant of tasks—can shift an unpleasant chore into a pleasant, or at least a neutral, one.

The Chores—Part II Mindful Break: How do you approach household chores? Are they dreaded undertakings full of grumbling, complaining, or accompanied by a long face? So much of our attitude depends upon the perspective we take.

First, set up the conditions for as much satisfaction as possible. Perhaps this means listening to a podcast with earbuds, blaring music so you can dance your way through the chores, or simply honoring the silence you crave. Keep an open mind and experiment with focusing on the sensations of cleaning, returning your focus over and over as your mind wanders.

If you are feeling a bit mischievous and your kids are around, another amusing tactic is to make it look like fun, like you are having the time of your life, in the hope they will ask to join in. Manipulative? Perhaps, but no real harm done, and in the process you may not find all the tidying so entirely unpleasant, yourself.

Self-Massage

Just to be clear and before you get any ideas, I'm not talking about that kind of self-massage. As Seinfeld would say, "Not that there's anything wrong with that." It's just that *Breathe, Mama, Breathe* isn't that sort of book. My apologies if it disappoints. Now that's out of the way. . . .

Before kids, you know, when I took for granted (because I had no idea) the luxury of time, my husband and I used to trade massages regularly. Divine. How cruelly paradoxical that *before* kids, when I was relaxed and mostly followed my own schedule and rhythms, is when I received calming massages regularly. Yes, we're all familiar with how adding an infant to our family affects our love (and massage) lives, at least for a while. *Ba bye, long, luxurious massage; hello, instantaneous sleep when allowed the rarity of lying horizontal.*

I began giving my daughter daily baby massages when she was an infant because I read it was a great way to bond and soothe. Over time, our massage slowly began to include a tune sung together—"We start with the back, the back, the back back back"—which also served the purpose of teaching her the names of various body parts. We continued this ritual right through her toddler and preschool years, when she would occasionally provide *me* with a baby massage. I wistfully recall those little hands gently rubbing my face, neck, and shoulders with such tenderness it was barely palpable, her way of extending to me a bit of that care and love. I don't remember exactly when she outgrew our ritual; it must have happened so gradually. *Sigh.*

> The factor that probably has the highest effect on outcomes for children is the level of well-being and functioning of their mother. If you care about children, take good care of mothers.
>
> —*Rick Hanson*

So, when my little guy was born, I was delighted to resume the practice on his new little frame, his face visibly relaxing as I placed the slightest bit of pressure on his temples and neck. When he became verbal, he sang right along with me and, just like his sister many years prior, he offers Mommy baby massages as well.

I should've known, though, that his version would veer dramatically from that of my daughter. No gentle, loving baby massage for me this time. My little guy instead gives me what he has named a rock 'n' roll baby massage. What in the world is that, you ask? That, my friends, is a warp-speed massage given while screaming like Ozzy Osbourne on too much caffeine. Not exactly relaxing, but it is hilarious and makes me cry with laughter every time, which is precisely what my little guy is going for. The difference in personalities of my two offspring is often astounding. And delightful. And it keeps me on my toes, because with a rock 'n' roll baby massage, there is a good chance I could suffer minor injuries in the process.

Thankfully, there is also such a thing as self-massage, which I was first introduced to at the end of yoga class in *savasana* (corpse pose). For those of you who don't know savasana, you should acquaint yourself immediately. Savasana is lying flat on your back with your arms and legs extended, practiced at the very end of class. Meant to allow the energy created in the previous poses to heal and revitalize, it is deeply restful with a pleasing sense of feeling like you earned it. One yoga teacher actually went around the room, gently massaging each student's neck, shoulders, and hands while we rested in savasana. Come to think of it, I'm surprised I didn't follow her home after class, begging to take up permanent residence in her family.

Not only does self-massage feel great, it can have other welcome side effects as well. Massage reduces pain, stress, and muscle tension and increases blood flow and healing. Just as we bring our attention to subtle body sensations when we sit to meditate formally, self-massage focuses our attention on specific areas, offers more familiarity with the areas in which we hold tension, and allows us to offer ourselves some much-needed TLC. I've offered this to my husband and kids; why not myself?

The Self-Massage Mindful Break: Beginning with your scalp, gently massage in small circles around your head, noticing any areas of tenderness. With your first two fingers, gently draw small circles on your temples, both forward and backward. Place gentle pressure on the bones surrounding your eyes and brows, moving down to the area of the cheeks where the upper and lower jaw meet. Next move to the top of the neck where the head rests on the spine and feel the bones that protrude slightly. Slowly massage down the neck, pausing to attend to any areas of tenderness. Experiment with the amount of pressure. Slide your fingers onto your shoulders, searching for knots and alternately applying pressure and releasing. As you massage, notice if your mind wanders, then return your attention to this offering of self-care. Just as you would with your little one, bring an attitude of love and appreciation for this remarkable body.

Self-massage can be practiced whenever you have a free moment at work, at home, while stopped at a traffic light, or while watching a movie with your kids. If you have little ones, they may even want to get in on the action. Who knows, maybe you'll receive your own version of a baby massage, rock-n-roll or otherwise. Enjoy.

Turn Your Head

It's 4 AM and I am strung out on sleep deprivation and the unrelenting cries of a colicky three-week-old baby with reflux. His tiny body is swaddled in my arms; I pace, I sway, I bounce, and eventually I cry, too. This is my second go-round with a newborn, and I am aware, somewhere in the recesses of my garbled mind, that this, too, shall pass. Oh, but it's challenging to hang on to that thought as this little creature once again begins to scrunch up his precious face and wail inconsolably for hours.

As an attempt to soothe him, I pull out the all the lullabies I can recall amid my hazy fog of exhaustion. I sing "Twinkle, Twinkle, Little Star" in a near whisper. He quiets for a few blissful seconds. I serenade him with "Hush, Little Baby," and he commences the wails once again. Then, in our time of mutual need and desperation, I begin to sing songs perhaps meant more to calm myself, the maxed-out mama desperate for sleep, for quiet, for relief. The lyrics offer a handhold onto which I can grasp. A lifeline of hope. An alternate perspective from the one mired in weariness and a feeling of utter helplessness. And so I sing a simple, soulful tune I've heard performed live in magic harmony by the trio Red Molly (written by Susan Werner):

May I suggest
May I suggest to you
May I suggest this is the best part of your life
May I suggest
This time is blessed for you
This time is blessed and shining almost blinding bright
Just turn your head
And you'll begin to see
The thousand reasons that were just beyond your sight
The reasons why
Why I suggest to you
Why I suggest this is the best part of your life[*]

My off-key voice, partially hoarse from exhaustion, cracks with emotion as the tears pool in my eyes and slowly spill down my cheeks. But I am smiling through the tears. The poetic lyrics have reconnected me with my strength. I have turned my head, and with the new perspective I see this precious little baby for what he is—nothing short of a miracle and one of the greatest blessings of my life. And I know, really know, that I will one day look back on this night with the bittersweet taste of nostalgia for

* © Susan Werner, 2001 (Frank Chance Music, ASCAP)

that profoundly intimate connection between mother and baby with struggle, song, and, finally, some soothing.

The Turn Your Head Mindful Break: When you find yourself seemingly stuck in a negative mood, an uncomfortable place, or a difficult situation, ask yourself, *Can I turn my head?* In other words, is there another way to view this situation, a broader perspective to take, perhaps filled with more awe and gratitude? We cannot force this shift in perspective, but we can offer ourselves the opportunity to step back and view the potential lessons available if we can remain curious. There is nearly always another way to view a situation if we can be open to it.

Sit

We all have our unique predispositions. It is helpful to be aware of yours so you can make small adjustments in a more mindful direction. Do you naturally suffer from low motivation? If so, perhaps this mindful break is not the one for you, and you'd benefit from the next, which gets you moving mindfully.

If you naturally overdo and find it challenging to just sit in the midst of a busy day, this mindful break is for you. Like a lot of busy moms I know, the only times you may actually sit are to chauffeur your children in the carpool, to use the bathroom (and if you have little ones, you are likely not alone), or at the end of the long, full day.

Amy, a stay-at-home mom, explains how this, for her, is a guilt-driven way of being. Somewhere along the way she internalized the pervasive cultural productivity message of all or nothing, that if she stops to take a load off for just a few moments, she must not be contributing her fair share. Mind you, I have never met a stay-at-home mom who spends her day sprawled on the couch munching bonbons, least of all Amy. But this is where the cultural message of productivity (read: *busyness*) gets it wrong. There is a huge difference between complete inertia and pausing for a few moments of stillness to recharge our batteries. But we often think and act as if there is no middle ground, and it may feel radical and wrong to do it any differently. This is not the truth, only pure cultural conditioning.

> Meditation is a fine-tuning device where we sit still and we tune and tune and tune until we get the most clear and still station on the dial, which is our soul.
>
> *—Elizabeth Lesser*

Michele, a work-outside-the-home mom, says that after returning home from work in the evening to a lively household, it seems as if there is not a moment to spare. "Sit down? Are you kidding me?" she laughs. I understand this misguided perception because, despite years of mindfulness practice, I can still find myself caught up in it. I also appreciate, from personal experience, the concern that sitting may induce near instantaneous sleep, another common side-effect of busy motherhood. To slow the chronic stress-perpetuating pace, however, we must learn to stop and sit because a bit of rest can be enough to recharge those batteries sufficiently for a while, promoting a much smoother, more enjoyable evening.

The Sit Mindful Break: If you are a constant mover, this might be quite challenging, but it's well worth the effort. Firmly but gently training ourselves to sit can feel much like training a rambunctious puppy that really wants to do the right thing but can't seem to keep still in spite of itself. It often takes the same bit of patience, good humor, and lots of treats. Find a comfortable spot to sit, ideally where you won't be interrupted or accosted for the next few moments. If it must take place in the middle of the chaos, so be it.

Take a few deep inhales and exhales, and let your shoulders drop. Relax your belly and legs and, if you'd like, allow the corners of your mouth to turn up in a hint of a smile. Notice the stillness. It might feel fantastic and luxurious. Perhaps the restlessness that drives us to get up and move is in full force, the pull to move almost more than you can bear. Like the energetic puppy learning a new skill, gently will yourself to sit through the desire to move. Kindly, but firmly, stay. This does get easier over time. Keep re-relaxing your body. Allow yourself the opportunity to rest and recharge. As you make your way into the next part of your day, notice if those batteries have a bit more life in them. Repeat as necessary.

Stretch

Having kids has either a) made me realize that I was always a morning person and just hadn't known it, or b) conditioned and brainwashed me so brutally to be a morning person that I now actually love it. Either way, I am up before dawn most days and, therefore, notice my overall energy level waning early in the afternoon. If I am at the office seeing psychotherapy clients for the day, there is little opportunity for movement, save for the hourly walk up and down one flight of steps to greet my next client. When I sense my energy flagging, I will often use the Stretch Mindful Break and am amazed at how it instantly wakes up my body and mind.

Mamas of newborns are also in need of mindful movement because they spend an inordinate amount of time looking down at the tiny babes cradled in their arms. As I carried, bounced, and rested my babies on my child-bearing hips, I tried valiantly to balance my body by alternating sides, but alas, it was like I had two left feet when it came to using my very-nondominant left arm. After my little ones were toddling on their own, it took months (and some help from yoga) for my body to regain its equal(ish) structural symmetry once again.

Settled at my computer for the writing of this book for hours at a time feels much like it did nursing my wee ones. Engrossed in the experience, time slips away. When I regain my awareness of what is happening around me, I am also keenly aware of the muscles in my neck and back that have gradually tightened and are begging to be lengthened.

Whether it's a nestled babe in my arms or computer keyboard under my fingers, there is the same slight forward curling around the focus of my attention, producing the need to step away, gaze upward, re-open my chest, pull my shoulders back, and rebalance my body. So whether you are in need of some energizing, lengthening, or balance, the Stretch Mindful Break will do you right.

The more we practice mindfulness, the more we become increasingly aware of our bodies and their subtle sensations and patterns. Our bodies *want* to move. Whether you are hauling a little one or a full laundry basket, or are perched at a computer for hours, your body will thank you for some movement in the form of a Stretch Mindful Break.

The Stretch Mindful Break: Stand up. Beginning with the head and neck, stretch each body part in turn, moving down the body until you have reached your ankles and feet. Circle the head slowly in both directions; then roll the shoulders forward and back. Raise your arms over your head and reach as high as possible, then slowly bend side to side. Honor your body and stretch only as far as is comfortable. Twist side to side at the waist, then hinge forward, allowing your head to hang freely. Circle the wrists and stretch the fingers. Squat up and down a few times to awaken the muscles of the upper and lower legs. Circle the ankles and flex and point the feet. After each body part has been attended to, briefly scan through the body again. Pause to notice any areas that are feeling especially tight, achy, or uncomfortable and spend another moment stretching those spots with care. When you are through, notice the level of energy in your body and mind. What has changed? Where? How? Remember, the more you treat your body with the respect and care it deserves, the more energy tends to increase. And we can all use more of that.

The Laundry

Confession: I don't hate laundry. This may sound blasphemous because the laundry seems to be such a formidable chore for most busy moms. But I never did receive that memo. Don't hate me for it. Perhaps it is because I rarely sort the clothes, just throwing it all in one load and hoping for the best. To me, laundry is a task that can be completed easily and in a short amount of time. Despite the fact that I do at least one load of laundry a day, I have actually always enjoyed it. Much like the growth chart on the wall in my little guy's bedroom, the size of the clothing in the laundry basket marks the growth and change of the composition of our family.

When my daughter was just born, I was in awe of those fresh-smelling little onesies and impossibly tiny socks. It was like watching time unfold as I sat down to fold her increasingly larger clothing that has now grown in size equal to my own. It's also now nearly impossible to tell whose clothes belong to whom (except for those size five jeans. I don't ever remember being a size five), and at long last we are finally at the point where we can share. Hooray!

Lately, it's my little guy's clothes that are the ones that seemingly grow in size overnight. As I sit and fold, my mind drifts off to the imagined future when the size of his clothes will rival those of my husband's, and I know the time will come all too soon. Pulled out of my reverie, I am grateful to return to the sight of those size fours that still wrap my little guy in freshly laundered love.

The Laundry Mindful Break: Allow these few moments of sorting and folding to be a pause in your day to take some deep breaths. Slow the pace just a touch. Feel the texture of each piece of clothing. Notice the pleasant scent of freshly laundered clothes (especially if you have a teenage boy—inhale that fresh scent now before it turns into that ubiquitous locker room scent). As you place the items into their respective piles, offer gratitude for each family member, sending him or her loving wishes as you do. Watch your thoughts and notice where they take you. There's no need to judge them—just watch and then come back to the tactile sense of the clothing. Rinse and repeat as necessary.

Yoga

No serious yoga practice occurs when my four-year-old is around. As soon as my yoga mat appears, he seems to think it is an unspoken invitation to use me like his personal human jungle gym. He just can't seem to help but get in on the action. Down Dog becomes London Bridge just begging to be climbed through and under. As I gaze toward the ceiling in Up Dog, a puckered kiss awaits. Cat-Cow pose soon morphs into a mommy horseback ride, and if there is any reclining on my back, he is soon poised and ready for an airplane ride.

And it's not just him. Apparently his toys love yoga as well. On numerous occasions while perched in triangle pose, my legs have been used as steeply inclined tracks for Thomas the Tank Engine and his sidekick, Percy. Matchbox cars have become painfully tangled in my hair, and I have drawn the line firmly with the headstand—do not mess with Mommy under any circumstances while she is upside down!

Sometimes we pull out our favorite musical yoga for kids CD by my wonderfully talented friend Kira Willey. If you haven't checked out her music, you must. A mindful mama herself, Kira writes music with that rare combination of appealing to both parents and kids. Her songs are accompanied by fun yoga poses meant to be performed to the music. My son knows all her lyrics by heart. I have an arsenal of memories tied to moving and dancing to her songs with both my children. A true gift.

> The question isn't so much, "Are you parenting the right way?" as it is: "Are you the adult that you want your child to grow up to be?"
>
> *—Brené Brown*

So, to get into a mindful yoga session and not fear grievous bodily injury while practicing, I do attend a weekly class. I also practice at home while the little guy is sleeping or otherwise occupied. Having long since given up on the expectation of any extended period of yoga practice in his presence, I am free to welcome the opportunity to practice together—playfulness, giggles, trains, and all. Although it's a much different practice with him around, I still manage to breathe deeply and stretch some tight muscles. I wouldn't trade it for the world.

The Yoga Mindful Break: I encourage you to try yoga both solo and with your kiddos. You will gain different benefits from each. If you have never tried it, I also encourage you to find a class with a knowledgeable instructor. Yoga is considered a moving meditation and is a great way to practice more mindfulness. Despite many novices' preconceived notions, you do not need to be flexible to do yoga. YouTube also has infinite instructional videos for all levels if a class is not possible in your immediate future. If it's challenging to find alone time to practice, kids can certainly be taught not to interrupt Mommy for a period of time. It is good modeling to show our kids the various ways we practice self-care.

Before you begin, ask yourself what is needed for you and your little ones in the moment. Is it some slow, calming poses or some vigorous, get-the-energy-out poses? Silence or music? Keep it fun and light. As you move your bodies, pause every so often to notice how body sensations have changed. Is your heart beating faster? Are you feeling warmer? Do you feel more energetic? Calmer? Is there a smile on your little one's face? If so, I'll bet there is one on yours as well. *Namaste* (from Sanskrit, "I bow to you" or "I bow to the divine in you.").

Cooking

In my early twenties, I regularly visited my childhood friend who had moved to Philadelphia for college. Frequenting the Greek restaurants on South Street, we dined on delicious authentic Mediterranean fare and admired the handsome dark-haired, olive-skinned men. I used to joke with her that I would die happy if I married a Greek man who could cook.

Well, as luck would have it, my hubby is half-Greek and a master in the kitchen (although somehow I am the one who makes the mean Greek spinach pie—guess I didn't specify that he needed to cook Greek food). I chose wisely; I am not the primary chef in our household. My husband has an uncanny ability to piece together a delicious meal with whatever ingredients already exist in the pantry. I, on the other hand, prefer to cook from a recipe and carefully planned-out ingredients. As a consequence, my family can just about guarantee that if Mom is in charge of dinner there will be some variation on salad, roasted veggies, pasta, and, of course, spanakopita or Greek spinach pie.

The Cooking Mindful Break: Perhaps you already enjoy cooking for your family. If this is the case, awesome, dive into this mindful break and enjoy. If, however, cooking feels like a necessary evil rearing its ugly head every afternoon at five o'clock (*Aaah, look at the time! What should I make for dinner tonight?*), experiment with this break and see if your attitude shifts at all.

As you begin to prepare a meal, take a deep breath and bring your full attention to the task. Perhaps notice what was required to bring the ingredients to your countertop—all the work that went into growing, harvesting, and transporting the food. You might offer gratitude for the privilege of plenty and the ability to nourish your family so easily. Think of feeding your family as one more way you can show your love for them.

As with all mindful breaks, this is not to be forced but is rather a subtle shift in our intention and awareness. Smell each ingredient and feel the texture as you wash, chop, and prepare. When your mind wanders, gently return your attention to the aroma or the appearance of the food. As you taste along the way, experience the flavors slowly, taking one mindful bite at a time. If you find yourself stuck in a rut preparing the same few meals week after week, consider attempting one new dish per week. Bring your curiosity and sense of adventure.

Of course, it's always an option to bring the kids in on the action because research shows kids eat a more variety of foods if they are involved in the preparation. It's probably not necessary to remind you that music and wine (for you) can be a welcome accompaniment. The bottom line is to mix it up, make it interesting, bring your full awareness to the process, and see what happens. *Kalí óreksi!* ("Enjoy your meal" in Greek.)

Got Muilt?

If you are a mom, I'll bet you've got muilt and plenty to spare. Mommy guilt is what I affectionately refer to as muilt. Much like the love for our sweet newborns, muilt follows the baby straight out of the womb and plants itself firmly into our hearts and minds. So whether you're a stay-at-home mom, a work-outside-the-home mom, or somewhere in between, you are bound to be carrying around some muilt.

The inner muilt critic is often at work whether we are conscious of her or not: *How are the kids? Am I doing enough? Am I doing too much?* We moms receive befuddling mixed messages about how to parent: *Don't miss a moment. Don't helicopter. Make the kids your highest priority. Your partner should come first. You can't have it all. Here's how to have it all. Don't forget your friends, career, volunteering, hobbies. . . .* Huh?

Don't get me wrong; a little guilt can be beneficial. Its presence can alert us if we have gone astray from how we want to be living. For example, when I become too consumed with work and the balance in my life feels off, a pinch of guilt allows me to reassess how I'm allocating my time as well as if I'm being present for my life. I schedule more time with my family, and, in doing so, immediately feel some relief, a clear sign that I am on the right path. If we use the guilt as a cue to gently shift the balance, we can thank it for the insight, let it go, and move on.

> Show me a woman who doesn't feel guilt and I'll show you a man.
>
> —*Erica Jong*

There are far too many occasions, however, when the guilt works overtime and shifts into muilt, which sounds something like this: *Wow, you've been distracted and working a lot lately. Great mom you are. Maybe you should take your own advice. You should definitely be more present. . . .* Most of us travel on plenty of unnecessary muilt trips, getting lost in self-blame and self-judgment, rarely acknowledging all our positive efforts and accomplishments. It's the muilt we allow to take up permanent residence in our minds that is unhelpful and counterproductive.

So how do we distinguish between a little instructive guilt and that fruitless mommy guilt? By homing in on our body sensations as cues. As our mindfulness practice develops we become increasingly aware of more subtle body sensations, which are ripe with information about our internal worlds if we are receptive to experiencing them. Quite often we are unaware of body sensations unless they are causing us marked discomfort. However, when we begin to pay closer attention, we recognize there are countless sensations that constantly ebb and flow.

Guilt is a signal, that, once heeded, sets us in the direction of our own intrinsic intentions rather than those extrinsically placed on us by society. Our bodies naturally begin to relax. We feel more at ease. There is a lack of unpleasant sensations. Muilt, in contrast, tends to stick around as shame that, rather than being instructive, becomes an ongoing inaccurate judgmental critique of our perceived inadequacies as a mom. Shame feels uncomfortable, often with a sense of nausea, unease, and muscle tension. Rather than urging us to act beneficially, muilt keeps us stuck.

When you have learned through consistent mindfulness practice how to get quiet, tune in to the inner voice guiding you, and heed it, that is all you need—you can let the confusing and often contradictory advice go and with it the mommy guilt. You know what is called for and you know you can trust it.

The Got Muilt? Mindful Break: When the guilt shows up and you realize, as we all do, that you have not been parenting the way you intend, judging yourself is a pointless exercise bound to keep you stuck. Instead, you might actually congratulate yourself for noticing where you have gotten off course and, with benevolence and encouragement, move in the direction of your intention.

Compassion and kindness are vital pieces of mindful awareness. Most of us give them away freely and easily but struggle with offering the same to ourselves. When you recognize you have fallen short, pick yourself up, dust yourself off, offer yourself some kind words, and simply begin again.

If the muilt is persistent and shaming, notice your thoughts about it. Is there some truth to it, or is it driven by our society's unrealistic expectations of how it believes you should parent? If the word *should* is part of the thought, most likely you have been taken for another ride on one of those unhelpful muilt trips. Remember, this parenting thing is hard. This balancing act is challenging. All we can do is our best. Get back on course, head in the direction of your parenting intentions, and leave the muilt behind.

Mommy High Fives

We've all heard the ubiquitous "good job!" uttered on the playground by beamingly proud parents each time their children make the slightest move. I have to admit I belonged to their tribe. Once considered a hallmark of attentive, tuned-in parenting, the constant "good job" is now considered over the top and slightly ridiculous in its frequency. As a first-time mom fourteen years ago, I wanted desperately to do this parenting thing right (read *perfectly*), so I followed the advice to praise my daughter's every accomplishment. As an excited new parent, I was amazed at each new milestone, believing that surely my daughter was advanced and a bit special.

At the time it felt natural and loving, but research has since shown that this blanket praise can backfire when it comes to our kids' internal motivation. Much has been written about how the "good job!" creates kids who expect praise for every little action, however common or uninspiring. We now know to praise the effort or the specific action itself, lest we encourage the development of a bunch of entitled, narcissistic little buggers.

Now that my daughter is older, I can see this effect with more clarity. Plus, I have to say I actually started to slightly annoy myself with the tiresome "good job." It feels much better to praise for the specific effort rather than for everything across the board. Let me tell you, it was nevertheless a hard habit to break and one that still arises on occasion with my little guy.

Well-placed and more carefully doled-out praise is healthier and, I would assert, comes easily and naturally for most of us in regard to our offspring. When it comes to praising ourselves as moms, however, it is a different matter entirely. In my experience working with moms, it's clear we are a self-critical bunch whose standards for our mothering are often nearly unattainable. The pressure that society (intentional or not) places on moms to be everything to everyone—while looking good, no less—can be seen on TV, in magazines, and with one click on Pinterest.

I say we need to "good job!" ourselves the way we once did our kids. Because we are typically so challenged by the unfamiliarity of treating ourselves in this loving way, a bit of over-the-top praise is usually just what the doctor ordered. Moms are also notoriously taken for granted (don't worry, this is just a phase that lasts only until your children have their own children—perhaps just another twenty-odd years or so); therefore, it can be empowering to do it for ourselves. Instead of the overused, somewhat cringeworthy "good job," I like to think of offering ourselves a big, fat Mommy High Five.

The Mommy High Fives Mindful Break: Whenever you accomplish something you may typically consider mundane and expected, such as checking a few things off your to-do list, offer yourself a mindful Mommy High Five. After you have made time for yourself to meditate, exercise, or any other form of self-care, a Mommy High Five is definitely in order. On occasion I will add a silent *Yes!* or *I rock!* to my self-praise. If this feels awkward, self-indulgent, or even a bit preposterous at first, I encourage you to keep at it for a few days as best you can with an open mind to see what unfolds. Moms I work with usually learn to love it. We are so good at noticing and acknowledging the accomplishments of others and woefully sad at praising our own. Just as you want to encourage positive behavior for your children, we moms are no different. When you move past the initial discomfort of the Mommy High Five, it will motivate continued healthy behavior and self-care—exactly what we wish to model for our children. So, high five to you, Mama. I guarantee you've already earned it.

Sick Days

There is a wise saying that we teach what we most need to learn. Absolutely. Why in the world do you think I've written this book, dear reader? Yes, of course I want you to learn how to infuse your life with mindfulness and reap all its wonderful accompanying benefits. But, if I am being completely honest with us both, I wrote it for myself as well. As a consistent reminder. Because I need it, too. You see, I am not always the best at heeding my own advice to slow down. It is an ongoing challenge for me. Mindfulness practice certainly supports slowing the pace to a sustainable speed and is just one of the many reasons I am drawn to it.

Katrina Alcorn, author of *Maxed Out: American Moms on the Brink*, writes about the common hospital fantasy in motherhood. Apparently there are plenty of moms who are so maxed out that the thought of being hospitalized actually sounds appealing. They do not wish to be laid up with some major illness, mind you, just sick or injured enough to grant them a few days of sleep and much-needed rest. Does this sound absurd to you?

Hmm, come to think of it, not only would there be undisturbed sleep, there would also be three square meals daily, delivered bedside. Eaten uninterrupted while lying down. On clean sheets. This is starting to sound tempting. Wait. Never mind, I'd have to be sick first. I think I'll pass.

If we refuse to rest until we are finished, we will never rest until we die.

—Wayne Muller

In all seriousness, I have to admit there was a time I was so sleep deprived that I, too, fell into this hospital fantasy camp. Perhaps you have been there, too. It's a poignant statement of our motherhood culture's impossible expectations that the hospital fantasy even exists at all. Clearly, many of us are in dire need of some rest, yet find it acceptable only if we are sick enough to be hospitalized. What?

I am not judging, just reacting, because again, I am guilty as charged. You see, I have a hard time offering myself permission to lie around on the couch watching movies unless I am, indeed, sick. It just seems like there are so many other important or worthwhile things to be doing instead. Why must I be under the weather before I deem it permissible to do nothing for the day? I, like the rest of us, am a work in progress.

And so, when a sick day in the form of a common cold inevitably rolls around, I try to embrace the forced slowdown. I try to acknowledge it as my body's way of letting me know I did not heed the previous warnings to slow my pace. I see a cold as not only an imposed period of rest I may not otherwise have taken but also as an opportunity to step back from the daily grind, offering time to reflect and gain a bit of perspective over my life.

The same goes for my kids' sick days. Depending on my workload for the day, I may initially grumble about the inconvenience of rescheduling eight patients to stay home with a sick child, accompanied by some guilt over last-minute cancellations. Soon enough, though, I am reminding myself how fortunate we are to be dealing with something so minor as a cold. I then begin to view the time as a welcome opportunity for extra cuddling, movie watching, and overall permission to do nothing. And it feels good to slow down, to be together with little expectation of crossing anything off the to-do list for the day. It's a shift in priorities and a shift in attitude. And despite the unpleasantness of headache and sore throat, it feels good. No hospital stay required.

The Sick Days Mindful Break: As best you can, see if you can welcome the occasional sick day (yours or your child's) as an opportunity to slow down and connect. Reassess your expectations for the day and prioritize only what is absolutely necessary. Crawl under the covers with a hot mug of tea, read that stack of magazines, or tune in to daytime TV. Resist the urge to be productive. Snuggle up to your child. Give in.

If you are fortunate enough to have a long stretch without being sick, try creating a sick day while feeling perfectly healthy. While enjoying good health, play out your day as if it were a sick day without all the snot and tissues. I think I'll give it a try, too.

Your Little Slice of Heaven

My mother-in-law's face has relaxed into a delighted, open grin as she canters gracefully past me atop her gentle horse. The memory itself is five years old; we lost her to cancer more than three years ago. The image, however, remains clearly etched in my mind, elicited as I watch my daughter confidently trotting her horse. My girl has inherited her grandmother's love of horses, both shared and nurtured by my sister-in-law. Accompanying my daughter's knitted brow as she concentrates on learning a new riding skill is the occasional glimpse of the same open grin her grandmother once wore.

As I sit back and watch, I easily recognize this as a moment of flow, a moment of joy—one of the only kinds of moments that really matter. It's a moment fostered by a combination of effort, challenge, and skill while engaging in something she loves.

Some of us know full well what brings us delight and have managed to hang on to it during the busy mothering days. Others are searching—either feeling we have left it behind with the carefree days before children or, perhaps, have never identified it at all. When I ask a fellow mom what she likes to do for fun, all too often her mouth falls slightly agape, she stares off into the middle distance, the sound of proverbial crickets filling the room, before looking at me with surprised dismay to say, "I have no idea." Life becomes so full that we sometimes forget to fill it with our own joy, but it's never too late to begin again.

> Nothing has a stronger influence psychologically . . . on children than the unlived life of the parent.
>
> *—Carl Jung*

I see it in my little boy's face as he runs uninhibited along a hiking trail, my husband as he is immersed in his music, and me—I feel the smile creep onto my face as I head out for an early morning ride on my bike. I love the strenuous effort of climbing the hills and the thrill of speed as I coast down the winding farm roads. I love the peace and quiet, Mother Nature all around. I love the warm, humid mornings, the crisp, fresh-air days, and the cold, glove-worthy ones. It's my happy place, my time to play and challenge myself.

My time on my bike is a sacred, renewing time for me. After less than an hour I return home happy, filled up, ready to dive into the day. My family easily senses the calm this time brings. I protect it for myself, for them, for the joy. It's a little slice of heaven.

May you find and nurture your little slice of heaven. May you make and protect the time. May you inspire and nourish your flow. And if you see me out on the road, I'll most likely be the one with the childlike grin on my face, pedaling with abandon.

The Your Little Slice of Heaven Mindful Break: If you are lucky enough to know what your passions are, take the time to make them happen and savor them. We need to set up the conditions to nurture more of these moments of flow amid our busy lives. Get your partner on board, hire a sitter, or swap babysitting with a friend. If it feels selfish to devote some precious time to your interests, perhaps revisit the Got Muilt Mindful Break (page 185).

If you are unsure what brings you into this state of flow, I invite you to notice the moments when you are smiling effortlessly. What did you love to do as a child? What did you like to do before kids? When did you lose track of time and were lost in the pure enjoyment of something? If it's not immediately clear, keep observing, keep challenging yourself, keep stepping out of your comfort zone. Flow will eventually show up. You will know it when you feel it. And when you discover, or reignite, what brings you a little slice of heaven, serve yourself up a healthy portion. You and your family will delight in the fullness it brings.

After the Meltdown (Yours)

Can you recall a time when you've lost it, screamed at your child, perhaps letting some choice words slip, causing tears and, worst of all, that wide-eyed, surprised look of fear in his eyes? You'd probably rather not remember. I get it. I feel the uncomfortable wash of shame just typing those words onto the page. I assume we've all been there (because I've never met a mom who told me she hasn't). There's nothing much worse for a parent as those few moments after you've royally blown it. Because regardless of how badly our kids are behaving, how irritating or maddening their attitudes, losing control of ourselves and the aftermath feels terrible for all involved. And if we aren't mindful about the way this plays out, we can stay stuck in that feeling, causing us to continue to act in hurtful ways, both to our families and to ourselves.

I now know myself well enough as a parent to recognize that my worst moments as a mom have come when I was both physically and emotionally spent. Exhaustion, coupled with feeling helpless in a situation, is an even more potentially treacherous combination for me. My son, who has historically not been a fantastic sleeper, recently went through an age-appropriate phase of waking more than once a night with typical fears and bad dreams. The first few interrupted nights I was lovingly reassuring and compassionate, a version of the soothing mommy I aspire to be. My husband dutifully takes his turns, but when I am awakened during the night (actually getting up to go to my son or not), my mind starts chattering and it takes time for me to allow it to settle and fall back asleep.

> Self-compassion is really conducive to motivation. . . . The reason you don't let your children eat five big tubs of ice cream is because you care about them. With self-compassion, if you care about yourself, you do what's healthy for you rather than what's harmful to you.
>
> *—Kristin Neff*

So on night three of intermittent rest, I had reached my limit. Instead of going to my little boy and gently reassuring him, I thoughtlessly embodied my scary mommy face and tone, frustrated words pouring out of me—"This is enough! We need to *sleep!*" Yes, this mommy on sleep deprivation can be a scary mommy. I am certainly not proud of that fact, but I own it because to own it means I recognize it and do my best to tread very lightly when those conditions arise. Unfortunately, there are nevertheless times when mindfulness slips away and I am caught up in my emotions and thoughts, reacting in ways that could easily induce a shame storm if I am not careful.

The difference between shame and guilt is that guilt is that sinking feeling we get in our guts in response to a behavior, whereas shame is that strong constellation of body sensations accompanied by a thought about who we are as a person such as, *What kind of mom are you anyway? A horrible one, apparently. Look what you've done.* Guilt highlights where we might want to change our behavior and, although uncomfortable, can then lead to improvement and growth. Shame, however, is often accompanied by strong body sensations such as a heavy pressure in the chest and a nauseating feeling in the belly as well as continued thought loops of self-recrimination. It's a powerful force, much like an out-of-control toddler in the midst of a tantrum, which can easily take on a life of its own if we aren't aware of it and know how to handle it with care.

In order to handle it with care, before anything else there needs to be a level of mindful self-awareness. WITH COMPASSION. Yes, I am shouting at you (lovingly—not with the scary mommy face). I emphasize WITH COMPASSION because I don't want you to miss that crucial piece. Awareness without self-compassion usually equals more shame. And the cycle continues.

When we allow ourselves to notice and accept the shame, however, it offers us the opportunity to forgive ourselves. This does not mean we get a free pass to continue down the same path next time, acting in the same unloving way. It's actually quite the contrary. This bit of self-reflection and care allows us a moment to take responsibility for our actions and perhaps construct a different, more compassionate way of handling the next similar parenting situation that arises.

Your meltdown, or misattunement, as Shauna Shapiro and Chris White call it, can be a valuable learning opportunity for your child as well. As they write in *Mindful Discipline: A Loving Approach to Setting Limits and Raising an Emotionally Intelligent Child*, "When we recover from misattunements—especially in emotionally turbulent times—and reconnect with our child, she develops the faith that it is possible to have disconnects and find our way back to love."

So back to my scary mommy tale. After I calmed myself with compassion, I enveloped that little guy in my arms, apologized for my actions, and began the work of forgiving myself, knowing full well the opportunity to try again will soon come. This is called working our parenting edge, that place where we stretch ourselves, where we freely acknowledge our imperfections, honor them, and promise ourselves and our kids we will do our very best to do better next time, and we mean it.

The After the Meltdown (Yours) Mindful Break: As is often the best place to start, take a few deep breaths, grounding yourself in the present moment (rather than in that negative thought loop in your mind). Feel the deep inhale and exhale as it fills and leaves your belly and chest. Notice the body sensations that are present. How would you describe the areas of the chest, the belly, and the head? What emotions are there—anger, sadness, shame? Now place your open hands over your heart, feel the warmth of your palms against your chest, and take another deep breath, breathing in the self-compassion and kindness this gesture offers. If this feels unnatural at first, that's fine. Notice that, too. For many of us it's often a foreign way of treating ourselves. It does get easier with practice.

Treat yourself as you would your children, with the knowledge that they are always learning and growing because the same goes for us parents. We are a work in progress. Some days you may feel raw, overwhelmed, and defeated. If you are stuck in one of those days, perhaps revisit the This, Too, Is Passing (page 126) and Mommy High Fives (page 188) Mindful Breaks, not to dismiss or avoid facing the aftermath of the meltdown but as a way to balance evenly those negative thoughts, emotions, and body sensations that can hang around for a while. Do the best you can to learn from your meltdown and move on. With mindfulness, we have the opportunity to start fresh in each new moment. Breathe and begin. . . .

Holidays

Whether it's birthdays, Christmas, Valentine's Day, or Halloween, most of us endeavor to create memorable holidays for our kids. Of course, we are saturated by the media with images of perfectly behaved, perfectly coiffed, and perfectly perfect families in all regards. It's tempting to get lulled into wishing for some of that, too. If the gorgeous family in that Target commercial can have a beautifully set dinner table (with very breakable china) adorned with delicious food and children who enjoy a leisurely holiday meal with smiles plastered on their faces (with apologies to Judy Garland), why, oh why can't I?

Oh, yeah, that's right, because my family is real, as in *imperfect*. And I embrace all our lovely imperfections and age-appropriate behavior. Well, at least I'm working on it. It essentially comes down to realistic expectations—lowering them, that is. Because after all, it's those unrealistic expectations rather than the conditions themselves that are the most disappointment inducing.

Take birthdays, for example. Although it's the custom in many cultures, I once believed it a bit self-indulgent to plan my own birthday, but after years of feeling slightly disenchanted by the day, I decided to take matters into my own hands. So a few years back I began scheduling the day off from work to create my own celebration. For me, it's not the gifts I value as much as how I spend my day—which is outside playing amid nature.

> To let go means giving up coercing, resisting, or struggling, in exchange for something more powerful and wholesome.
>
> *—Jon Kabat-Zinn*

My husband voluntarily joins me for what he now refers to as the semiannual "try to kill your husband day." (We also celebrate our wedding anniversary this way—hence the semiannual.) It's not as frightening as it sounds. Simply put, we head out in the early morning for a long trail run/hike and bike ride until we are spent, and then we savor a late lunch before returning home to the kids. Later that evening comes a home-cooked dinner by my culinarily talented husband, shared with our small extended family, followed by a trip to the local ice-cream shop (where I have also learned to BMOC—bring my own candle) so my family can sing "Happy Birthday" to their tired but delighted mom.

The Holidays Mindful Break: First and foremost, lower those expectations. Everyone will benefit from a loosening up, including you. Be aware of what is under your control and what is not. Plan as best you can—don't wait around hoping someone else might read your mind and then let it play out however it may. When you find yourself becoming tense or irritated by someone's behavior that does not meet your preconceived ideals, see if you can be open to and accept the imperfections of the person, of the day, of the event. Often when we look back on these times, it's the most imperfect moments that hold the most loving sense of nostalgia. As best you can, set up the conditions and then let the rest take care of itself. Sit back, breathe, watch, take part, and enjoy. Target can do it its way—you do it yours.

CHAPTER 5

Connecting with the World

This chapter includes mindful breaks meant to strengthen your optimism, gratitude, and awe muscles by connecting with nature, others, and ourselves in a more mindful, loving way. Experiment with bringing your mindful practice out into the world at large. Be ready and open for how it expands your heart and your regard for those you encounter.

Gratitude

Along with my adolescent daughter's growing independence, selfies, and flatiron, the expression "attitude adjustment" has been making a recent appearance in our household. When a hint of teenage insolence creeps into the conversational tone, my husband and I provide a cautionary reminder of respect. Although essentially unacceptable, I expect a bit of defiance, and at times I'm secretly amused by its dramatic and cynical quality. How humbling to remember that my attitude is occasionally in need of an adjustment as well.

A reader of the *New York Times Motherlode* blog recently asked why it seems today's parents complain so much about parenting: "Do any of you ever enjoy the daily lives you have chosen? Because it sure doesn't sound like it." I sat up straight and proceeded to take a bit of personal inventory. Is writing about mindful motherhood perceived as whiny and complaining? How does this negative bent play out in my own family life? A provocative question of parenting perspective, it brought to mind the times I have taken so much for granted and the simple ongoing Gratitude Mindful Break I use as an antidote to complacency.

> That joy that doesn't depend on what happens is the joy that springs from gratefulness.
>
> *—Brother David Steindl-Rast*

I like to practice gratitude at the end of my formal meditation because that is when I am typically more open hearted and calm. Over time, I have watched it subtly shift my perspective. From something as simple as a hot cup of coffee to something as precious as my children's good health, bringing my attention to what I hold dear has a way of allowing me to relish it and appreciate it even more throughout my day. I have noticed other positive effects from this mindful break as well. Things I once may have quickly glossed over with barely a shrug, such as watching my husband interact with our children, now beckons me to pause briefly and take notice.

Our teenage daughter still enjoys curling up next to her dad on the couch to watch a movie. I take comfort in their continued bond because I know he is, and always will be, her first role model for a loving relationship. She glows with pride after finishing a long run with, and encouraged by, him. Our little guy loves to rock out with his dad on guitar while he bangs away on the drums. Our kids are fortunate to have such a loving, affectionate, playful dad. Acknowledging these heartwarming moments automatically strengthens my love and appreciation for him. It's an effortless win-win.

We all are in need of an attitude adjustment occasionally. Regularly practicing gratitude organically encourages us to enjoy the daily lives we have chosen, acting less like dissatisfied teenagers and more like the mindful moms we aspire to be.

The Gratitude Mindful Break: Whether you add this mindful break to the end of your five-minute guided meditation or as a stand-alone mindful break during the day, first pause and take a few deep breaths. Ask yourself what it is you are grateful for right now and see what arises. Notice any accompanying body sensations. If your thoughts begin to veer off into negativity, gently redirect them back to gratitude for these few moments. It's important that you do not allow or force this practice to become about that for which you feel you *should* be grateful. There is no right or wrong. What shows up may be predictable or may surprise you. It's OK if your gratitude favorites play out day after day as long as you feel genuinely connected to them. Also see if you can find something new or novel to appreciate each day. Strengthen and stretch that gratitude muscle.

Practice this mindful break daily for a month and you will notice a positive shift in your level of ongoing appreciation. Research shows that as we practice gratitude, we are training our minds to notice more of the good already out there in the world. Notice it, savor it, and share it with your kids. Plant those seeds, water them, and watch your gratitude grow.

Unpleasant Moments

Can you guess the life span of an emotion—how long a feeling sticks around after it has arisen? Ninety seconds. Tell that to my emotions, though, because they often act as if they've never received the memo. Ninety seconds. Hard to believe? It was for me, too.

Jill Bolte Taylor, PhD, neuroanatomist and author of *My Stroke of Insight,* found that the natural life span of an emotion is only a minute and a half. According to my estimation, this means the average time it takes for an emotion to move through the nervous system and body is about equivalent in length to a labor contraction. Depending upon the circumstances, our emotions can feel just as fierce. Our emotions are also similar to labor contractions in that they build, crest, and then abate. I find this to be an incredibly comforting and helpful reminder in the midst of an emotional storm. We can, after all, tolerate most anything for ninety seconds.

But herein lies the rub. The emotion will subside only if we don't add fuel to the (possibly already raging) fire. In eastern philosophy this is referred to as shooting the second arrow. The first arrow is the challenge that life hands us, that which is not under our control. The second arrow is shot when we heap additional suffering on top of the original hurt.

> Life is painful.
> Suffering is optional.
>
> —*Sylvia Boorstein*

Here's an example. As I sit to write on a bright winter Sunday afternoon, we here in the Northeast are clearing out from a record snowstorm, a blizzard that began Friday evening, slowly abating twenty-four hours later, unloading a whopping thirty inches of snow in that time. With winds at forty miles an hour and temperatures near zero, there was none of the typical frolicking outside during this storm. My family was, therefore, all tucked inside the house together for a fairly long stretch of time, at least by our usual standards of daily fresh air and outdoor play. Three of us with colds, one of us with a four-year-old's infinite amount of energy to burn, one of us a teenager with little tolerance for said four-year-old's energy, one of us outside much of the day battling snow with plow and shovel, and one of us with a looming manuscript deadline. *Gulp.*

You see, I usually spend a good part of Saturdays writing in my quiet therapy office, but I soon altered my expectations of leaving the house upon waking to a foot of snow outside my window. So, after a leisurely breakfast, I retreated to my home office (inconveniently located in the middle of the bustling house), hoping to spend some concentrated time writing. I figured if I could get just two hours in, I'd be able to relax and enjoy the rest of the snowed-in day with my family. A great plan, in theory. However, some hours and countless disruptions later, I was a grumbling, frustrated mess of a mom. By mid-afternoon, I had not written one good coherent sentence, nor had I been fully present with my family at any point throughout the day. I was distracted, grumpy, and very unpleasant to be around. I knew it, but I had a hard time stopping it, which only led to more frustration.

The first arrow in this scenario was my inability to find focused writing time amid the pressure of an upcoming deadline. Somewhat unpleasant, yes, but had I used an Unpleasant Moments Mindful Break (pages 214–15), I would have been looking only at those ninety unhappy seconds. Doable. Done.

Unfortunately, I didn't catch it in time, thereby automatically shooting the second arrow (and third, fourth, and fifth). The second arrow is the story we tell ourselves about the challenge. It is the dialogue, the judging, and the resistance we add to an already-painful situation that keeps us stuck in that emotional storm. Therefore, my thoughts looked something like this as I endured interruption after interruption: *You want another hot chocolate? You're hungry again? What the *&^. I need to get to my computer. This is not working! You need to learn to play on your own. NO MORE TV!* And on and on. Although I may not have spoken those actual words aloud, my family received the general message loud and clear. You get the picture.

Do you think I was being ridiculous and overdramatic? I was, and we do it all the time. Just watch your mind do its thing the next time a difficulty presents itself. It is a humbling part of the human condition.

When we recognize the second arrow, name it, *allow* it (it is already here, you might as well), and are curious about it, we completely change its hold over us. In retrospect, I should have named the pressure and frustration, noticed it with some self-compassion, and then let go of my writing expectations for the day as soon as it was apparent I would not be leaving the house. This would have freed up my attention and energy to relax into really being with my family. Ninety seconds. No second arrow. So much better.

This, of course, in the big scheme of things, is an example of a minor unpleasant situation. But what about those *really* unpleasant moments—the ones that are terrifying, heart wrenching, or rage inducing? How do we work with those? What if it feels too overwhelming? Too intense? Actually, we work with them in much the same way.

First of all, there is always the breath, which is one of the reasons we use it as a common point of focus for meditating. It can serve as an anchor for our attention, not to avoid the intense emotions but rather to calm ourselves enough so we can face the unpleasant feelings. I liken it to working with the breath during childbirth. Because labor contractions are so incredibly powerful, it is easy to get lost in their intensity. When we maintain a point of focus, such as the breath, it allows us to hang on long enough until the contraction subsides once again. When we remind ourselves that the intensity will pass if we can breathe, relax our bodies, and stay focused on the inhale and exhale, we have the ability to ride out any emotional storm.

The Unpleasant Moments Mindful Break: If you are facing a minor unpleasantness, be on the lookout for what body sensations tend to arise when conflict occurs. Almost like our own little warning system, we all have a unique pattern that can be helpful to identify so we can more easily catch what is coming. Can you be aware of your pattern in the future? When you notice unpleasant body sensations arise, bring your full attention to them, observing the subtleties that comprise them, noticing how they change, if they change. Doing so certainly doesn't take the unpleasantness away, but it allows us to pause and choose how we wish to respond to the challenge.

When the situation you are facing is more intense and overwhelming, first remind yourself that if you can gently keep your focus on the body or breath, this emotionally intense storm will last only ninety seconds. As best you can, take a few long, deep breaths, relax your body, and bring your attention to the breath. Ground yourself in the feeling of the inhale and exhale. Let it anchor you. Rather than resist the intense emotions, which is often our natural response to something unpleasant, see if you can work on accepting them. Please know that accepting does not equal condoning or inviting. But whether we like it or not, those feelings are here. Can you allow yourself to face and feel them? The more you remain aware and calm, the sooner the storm will pass. You may feel some residual unpleasantness, to be sure, but you will now be more able to tolerate and choose how to respond to it.

Offer yourself plenty of compassion with this mindful break. It is the practice of a lifetime and deserves plenty of patience and respect. May you find comfort in its usefulness. May the second arrow remain untouched in your quiver.

Delighting in the Senses

I'm not sure about you, but I find myself bursting with energy and optimism with the arrival of spring. Living in the chilly winter climate of the Northeast, it's like my senses have been hibernating as I walk outside and am struck by the warm sunshine, birds chirping, flowers and grass slowly reappearing; my senses are suddenly on high alert.

Daily throughout the year, weather permitting, I pack my son into the stroller and head out on the same rural walking route. Some days I find myself lost in thought, on automatic pilot, barely aware of time passing. Yes, we've gotten our daily dose of fresh air, exercise, and vitamin D, but, sadly I have missed an opportunity to savor Mother Nature's abundance.

Today, however, I deliberately focused my attention on the emergent hints of spring all around me. My son was happy to oblige. While tuning into our sense of hearing, this is just a smattering of what we observed: a robin's song, a rooster's caw, a woodpecker's thrumming, a dog's bark, a stream's gurgling, and an airplane's droning overhead. It was delightful and transformed what might have been an ordinary hike into a feast for our senses.

> Those who bring sunshine into the lives of others cannot keep it from themselves.
>
> —*James M. Barrie*

Quite effortless after a long, harsh winter, this concentrated attentiveness is mindfulness in action and feels much like seeing the world with a fresh perspective. Maintaining this keen awareness becomes increasingly challenging as we grow older and busier and as the warmer weeks wear on. We take for granted the verdant landscape and sunshine as our bodies and minds acclimate. We do, however, have a choice whether to continue to live on autopilot or stop and literally smell the roses. So, whenever possible, get outside and delight in your senses.

The Delighting in the Senses Mindful Break: Regardless of the weather or season, step outside for a few moments and take in the sights as if you have never noticed them before. Simply observe. Listen mindfully to the sounds all around you. Can you hear noises near and far? Is there any sort of silence? What about smells? Are they unpleasant, pleasant, or neutral? Notice the temperature and other sensations. Do you feel the warmth of the sun? The dampness of rain? The charge in the air before an impending storm? Make sure you get the kids in on the action as well. Challenge them to notice and report as many observations as possible. As this mindful break becomes a habit you may be surprised at how much more of your life you are really living fully aware, enjoying your surroundings with a renewed appreciation and sense of awe.

Good Enough

Letting good enough be good enough. Letting go of perfection. This one is so hard for most of us, and, well, why wouldn't it be? Raising our children is often the most important endeavor we will ever undertake, so of course we take it seriously. I think this is especially hard for first-time moms.

When I was pregnant with my daughter, I read everything under the sun about parenting, wanting to feel prepared and in control as much as possible. As we all know, nothing can completely prepare us for parenthood. I put so much unnecessary pressure on myself to make the right decisions that I ultimately realized were inconsequential. The self-imposed pressure made me more anxious than I needed to be and less able to simply enjoy her.

Busy moms are notorious for taking on too much. The pressure we place on ourselves is enormous. Whether working outside the home or within, most women believe they should be able to offer their children plentiful opportunities, entertain them much of the time, keep the house in order, maintain strong relationships with partners and friends, prepare the best snacks (read *creative* and *healthy*—thanks for that, Pinterest) for the classroom party, and volunteer, all while looking fit and young, with beatific smiles plastered permanently on their faces.

> The thing that is really hard, and really amazing, is giving up on being perfect and beginning the work on being yourself.
>
> *—Anna Quindlen*

Reinforced by social media and our fast-paced society, it's easy to buy into the illusion that everyone else has it all together. Many busy moms suffer from a form of the "imposter syndrome," a false belief that others are more competent and that our gross ineptitude will eventually be discovered. The truth is we all have times when we feel capable of juggling our many roles and times when it feels as if it could all come crashing down at any given moment. In *Maxed Out,* Katrina Alcorn quotes a friend: "The line between 'Everything's okay' and 'I'm on the verge of total collapse' is so thin. . . . All it takes is one thing too many. . . . One nudge in the wrong direction, and everything comes tumbling down." Attempting to maintain the ideal façade ultimately leads to one or more of the following: burnout, apathy, depression, anxiety, and struggling with consistent feelings of never-quite-good-enough.

When we realize that despite outward appearances no one is doing it all alone, without help or without eventually crashing and burning at some point, we can work toward liberation from our society-reinforced, unrealistic expectations. I have lightened up over the last fourteen years as I see my daughter is turning out (so far) just fine, but I still struggle with this one occasionally. I often tell moms who are so tough on themselves that good enough is great. Perfectionism and unrealistic expectations of ourselves, our spouses, and our children get us nowhere fast.

The Good Enough Mindful Break: Notice when those perfectionistic thoughts arise, attempting to convince you that you, your perceived performance, or your kids on their own are not enough. Perfectionism is often accompanied by tense muscles and an overall lack of enjoyment. Can you let go of those expectations just a bit? Test it out when possible. Often we come to see that those stressful details really didn't matter and that we were able to enjoy and be more present because of that bit of letting go. With compassion, remind yourself that for much of the time good enough is great. Keep working at it. It takes practice and patience, but it's so worth the effort. From one recovering perfectionist to (perhaps) another, trust me on this one.

Don't Know

In *Year of Yes*, Shonda Rhimes shares her thoughts about raising three daughters: "Before kids, my confidence could not be dented. Now it's shattered on a daily basis. *I don't know what I am doing*. There is no manual. There's no checklist."

Oh, dear. If Shonda Rhimes, brilliant mind that she is, doesn't know what she's doing, what does that portend for the rest of us? Unsure whether to take solace in this or turn and run for the hills, I am at least comforted by the reinforcement that we are all seemingly in the same bewildered mothering boat.

Although bewilderment is an innate part of the mothering condition, from all outward appearances it seems to be happening only for me. Too often it sure looks like everyone else has it all together. It helps to know I am not alone, which normalizes my mothering experience and helps me appreciate that at some time or another we all feel as if we have no idea what we are doing.

Another reason I am such an advocate of speaking our truth and owning our imperfections is that it frees us up to have honest, lifesaving conversations with other moms who have been there or who are now fighting the same good fight right alongside us.

Whether we're decoding a newborn's cries or considering an appropriate teen curfew, we are often entering unfamiliar territory. Even if we have been around the block with older children, all kids come with their own unique sets of characteristics, personality traits, and behaviors, potentially causing us to feel the same amount of uncertainty as if it were our first go-round.

> Be who you are and say what you feel, because those who mind don't matter and those who matter don't mind.
>
> *—Bernard Baruch*

When my son was born ten years after my daughter, I unexpectedly found myself right back in that familiar, helpless place of having no clue what he needed as he wailed for hours. Because I am a doer, my inability to solve the problem was what I found most distressing. I would run through the obvious checklist hoping for a quick fix: *If he's wet, great,* I thought, *I can change him. If he's hungry, OK, I can take care of that, too. Tired, no problem.* But the relentless, mind-numbing cry, simply because he seemed to wish he could climb back into my quiet, warm uterus for a while, *that* was causing me a great deal of anxiety.

I recall my little guy's one-week well visit. Feeling utterly defeated, I told our kids' pediatrician, whom I trust, respect, and had known for more than a decade, that I could not distinguish between his cries. It all sounded maddeningly the same. She tried to affectionately Spockify me, claiming, "You know more than you think you do," but I wasn't buying it. I looked her dead in the eyes (with my bloodshot ones) and said, "No, I really have *no idea*." Of course, after another week or so I did know which differentiated cry expressed hunger, sleepiness, or the need for a diaper change. But, under those former conditions, a week is a very long time.

Fortunately, mothering does not feel this perplexing all the time. There are plenty of spells when it feels like I am coasting blissfully, having figured things out for a while. I enjoy it while it lasts because I know that another learning curve is waiting for me right around the corner.

If we can accept that *I have no idea* is a natural component of parenting, there is a bit of relief in it. There is some freedom in not knowing, in not needing to have all the answers immediately instead of pausing, checking your gut, and perhaps even waiting it out. My fantastic pediatrician and Dr. Spock are right. We do know more than we think we do. But sometimes we need to settle into not knowing for a while first because, despite her apparent maternal self-doubt, if Shonda Rhimes can create such brilliant, authentic characters and story lines, she must also have some idea of what she is doing as a mom. There is hope for us all.

The Don't Know Mindful Break: Not only is it invaluable to model honesty with other moms, it can also be wonderfully instructive for our kids as well. As children request increasing independence, it's OK, and often advisable, to answer, "I don't know. Let me think about it, and I'll get back to you." This not only demonstrates that we take their requests seriously, but also it models owning uncertainty, imperfection, and the disciplined skill of pausing to gather thoughts rather than reacting immediately and impulsively.

It first helps to recognize when we have moved into unfamiliar territory and admit to an *I don't know* moment. This is harder for some of us than others. By definition, *accepting* means reconciling to, and no longer resisting, the situation. We can be open to learning, to experimenting, to trusting our intuition, but first we need to relinquish control. *I have no idea.* Name it for yourself. With compassion. No need for shame. Remember, we have all been there (or are there right now). Talk with other moms. Ask questions. Share your stories. Relish the journey and all that we learn about ourselves and our kids along the way.

The In-Between Moments

Imagine you were told you had only six months to live. What would you do with the time? If you pause and reflect for a moment, things quickly become clear. Our answers will differ to some degree based upon our unique personalities and passions. If you are an adventurous soul, you might imagine traveling or addressing some of those lingering bucket-list items. Perhaps you would make amends with someone important to you. Maybe you would ensure that your loved ones understood exactly how much they mean to you. One thing I imagine we would all do more of is simply be with our family and friends. Just hang out. Talk about important things. Truly listen to one another. Hug. Hold hands. You know, the completely ordinary in-between moments we tend to either rush through or not allow time for at all when life feels so busy and overscheduled.

It's illustrative, isn't it, when we pause and contemplate it. Not to sound macabre, but the truth is that not one of us really knows how much time we have. Not that I suggest you live in constant fear of this truth, but rather that you use it as a reminder every so often to come back to your deepest-held values and priorities. I do understand that we cannot relinquish all responsibilities and schedules. However, when we are rushing from one activity to the next, there is no in-between because any interim time is consumed with thoughts about what is next to come. What if we slow the pace a bit and pay more attention to those in-between moments so easily lost amid the busyness? Even better, what if we create more in-between moments and bring our full attention to them?

> Time stands still best in moments that look suspiciously like ordinary life.
>
> —*Brian Andreas*

In-between moments can be opportunities ripe with potential for connection, for creativity, for thought. If it currently seems there are few of them in your day, you are either attempting to squeeze too much into a given amount of time or you are so distracted by ticking items off your mental to-do list that you do not recognize those in-between moments when they present themselves.

Our minds also benefit from a bit of time to process the constant flood of incoming stimuli. With more in-between moments comes increased space to be kinder, more thoughtful, more creative, and certainly more present. When I'm in a hurry, I'm inherently acting with less kindness. I miss the opportunity to smile and look someone in the eyes while walking down the street. I miss the chance to have an interesting conversation with my fellow mom standing in front of me in the grocery line. I miss the opportunity to prioritize what is most important, what was so clearly clarified in the six-months-to-live exercise.

It's in the in-between moments when I have also had the most rewarding conversations, the most creative aha moments, and the greatest sense of gratitude. They are those ordinary times when it seems like nothing much is happening, but when we bring our full awareness and curiosity to it, we see that everything is happening: while relaxing on my bed, engaged in thoughtful conversation with my teenage daughter; after dinner, when my husband and I linger for a few moments at the table to talk and laugh. Those are the unplanned moments I walk away from feeling connected, nourished, understanding, and understood. Requiring only a small amount of time, they are precious when held in the framework of whittling down to what matters most.

The In-Between Moments Mindful Break: Take a few breaths, close your eyes, and reconnect with what arose for you as you imagined the six-months-to-live scenario. What images appeared? Which people? What thoughts and emotions? These are priorities. If at all possible, make more of what you imagined happen. Start small but be deliberate about it. Come from a place of love and appreciation for what matters most to you.

Can you be on the lookout for those in-between moments you might have normally glossed over? Create more space in your day for those brief pauses where seemingly nothing is happening. When you recognize one, take a few deep breaths and bring your sense of curiosity to it. What body sensations are present? Is there a sense of ease in the body? If you are with someone else, can you offer him or her your full attention? If you notice impatience or restlessness arise, can you simply stay in spite of the pull to get on to the next thing? As best you can, continue to set up the conditions for more in-between moments; then let go of expectations and see what they bring you.

CHAPTER 6

Ending the Day

Wine

I promised you in the Coffee Mindful Break (pages 54–55) that the evening Wine Mindful Break would come. Were you waiting for it? Can't say I blame you. Both coffee and wine are occasionally used as my choice mommy survival tools. These two beverages hold a special place in my heart. Therefore, I am somewhat finicky when it comes to them, not because I am a sophisticated oenophile properly quaffing an exclusive vintage, but simply because I am a lightweight, a cheap date if you will, able to consume only one glass before I become tipsy. So, naturally, I want to savor that single glass.

A connoisseur I am not—my only real education an eight-week wine appreciation seminar during senior year of college (Sign me up, please. No credits, but, seriously, who cares?). Each week we tasted and discussed numerous types and varietals of wine from diverse regions around the world. It was entertaining and enlightening to hear fellow class participants' unique descriptions: pear, mushroom, oak, citrus, chewy, light, full bodied. The final class was an elaborate dinner where each student prepared a course to be paired with carefully selected wine. The only thing

I remember clearly was the dessert course: double-layer chocolate fudge cake with a beautiful red dessert wine. I recall thinking I had died and gone straight to vino heaven (although, come to think of it, I must've certainly been inebriated by that point).

Anyway, I digress. The point is that you obviously need not be an expert to bring your full awareness and sense of curiosity to your full goblet. Whether sharing a leisurely dinner with friends or sipping a glass solo while preparing dinner, you can practice, and delight in, your own unique version of Wine Mindful Break.

The Wine Mindful Break: If you are with others as you partake, you may want to include your companions in your Wine Mindful Break. If not, go ahead and secretly enjoy your mindful glass of wine. If yes, perhaps, much like my edifying college class, you would like to debate your beverage observations with your companions. Who cares if you know what you are talking about and what specific language to use? Have fun and be as creative as possible with your descriptions.

In either case, take a deep breath in and out, bringing your full attention to that lovely beverage in front of you. First notice the color of the liquid settled in the glass. Gently swirling it in a circle, observe the density of it. Next, bring the glass to your nose and breathe in, inhaling the inviting scent. Taking your first sip, let the wine rest in your mouth for a few seconds, allowing the time to fully taste its complexity. Slowly swallow, noticing any tastes or scents that linger afterward. Maybe you'd like to silently offer gratitude for the wine itself, imagining all the effort, labor, and energy that went into bringing it to your table. Using the wine as your point of focus, each time your mind wanders off in thought, gently return your attention to the delicious nectar of the gods in front of you. *In vino veritas*. Cheers.

[Note: As a therapist, I am sensitive to those of us for whom alcohol is a dangerously slippery slope. I would be remiss if I did not mention that if your consumption of wine, or any other substance for that matter, has become a concern for either yourself or a loved one, please seek help and, of course, skip over this mindful break. Please drink responsibly. I mean it. (Now I do sound like a mom.)]

Dishes

If you've let your family in on your growing mindfulness practice (and I encourage you to do so), you can share the Dishes Mindful Break as an example of bringing your full awareness to any activity, even one as mundane as dishwashing. Before the washing commences each evening, you may want to assess what feels most needed for you in that moment.

For example, if there are little ones you have cared for and scampered around with all day, you might benefit from quiet, reflective dishwashing time for Mommy. On the other hand, little ones often love to help wash the (unbreakable) dishes, which can keep them occupied as you tidy up the kitchen. If your kids are older and rarely make an appearance outside their bedrooms except to be fed and when a ride is needed, another option is to jointly wash and dry; conversation tends to flow more freely when our teens are engaged in a communal task. If it works with your family's logistics, it can also be a great opportunity to catch up with your spouse as you work together rather than dividing and conquering the household chores separately.

The Dishes Mindful Break: If you are sudsing it solo: Take one big breath in and out. Check in with your posture, perhaps rolling the shoulders back and standing taller. As you turn on the faucet, bring your full attention to the sensation of touch and the feel of the water as it glides across your skin. Take in the clean scent of the soap. Bring awareness to the temperature, the texture and feel of the heavy dishes, the soft sponge, and the smooth water. Slow things just a notch from your typical pace and be as fully present with your senses of touch and smell as possible, letting them become your primary focus. Your mind will do its thing and wander off, perhaps to the next few items on your to-do list or a conversation engaged in earlier. When you realize you have wandered off in thoughts, gently return your attention to the dishes and your senses. You will need to do this repeatedly, and that is perfectly fine.

You also might wish to spend a moment imagining all the dishes washed over hundreds of years all over the world. Allow it to be a moment of reflection for the necessity, commonality, and simplicity of this universal task, a simple way to restore a bit of order and cleanliness to our lives. Perhaps offer gratitude for this brief time of quiet and opportunity for a mindful break.

If this is a joint effort: Following the guidelines above for solo sudsing, begin by bringing your awareness to the sense of touch and smell. If the conversation is flowing, allow the point of focus to be your dishwashing partner rather than your senses. When your child or spouse is speaking, pause and look the speaker in the eye every so often, noticing your body sensations as you take in the words. As best you can, see this as an opportunity to connect mindfully rather than as one more task to be completed as quickly as possible. Really be there for both of you. It's in these everyday moments that we can encourage space for sharing, for connecting, and for time to simply be together.

Bath Time

When my daughter was a wee one and before I began practicing mindfulness, I lived much of the time in get-'er-done land. My mindset was all about how much I could accomplish in a certain amount of time. Whether it was chores around the house or the bedtime routine, the pace often felt urgent and hurried; it was all about checking things off the list as quickly and efficiently as possible. Looking back, I imagine my little girl must've felt like she was being run through the speedy car wash during bath time each night: Suds her up, scrub her down, give her a good rinse, spring out of the tub, towel her off, into those jammies, and off to the bedroom you go. Yes, folks, we've just hit a new world record. Hooray! What sort of world record I was trying to beat, I have no idea—the one in my own head, I guess.

I still enjoy visiting this land of efficiency and productivity, but I am now much more apt to notice when I am hanging out there—perhaps looking around and taking in the sights (while quickly crossing some items off the list)—rather than living there permanently without ever noticing my surroundings. Because when we are immersed in the land of productivity, it leaves very little room for being in the moment, for the opportunity to appreciate all that is right in front of us. Pardon the pun, but it's so important that we soak it up while we can.

Experience is that marvelous thing that enables you to recognize a mistake when you make it again.

—F. P. Jones

Many years later, I now know how quickly bath time becomes a remnant of the past, replaced instead with unbelievably long showers of the teenage years, when privacy reigns and you notice one day with astonishment that your once-wee-one walks out of the bathroom in a fluffy robe cloaking her full-fledged grown-up body. *Whoa . . . when did that happen?*

And so I am now more apt to linger over my little guy's bath, playing along with whatever water game he has concocted that evening. For I know one day in the not-too-distant future that this, too, will be a relic of his much-too-short-lived bath time past.

The Bath Time Mindful Break: Whenever possible, carve out enough time for the bath to be a slow, relaxing experience for both of you. Take a few deep breaths. Take in the warm, moist air through your nostrils, notice the scent of bubble bath or baby wash. Acknowledge the miracle of that little naked body that seems to grow (and often actually does) overnight. Feel the warm water as it moves through your fingers, the soft washcloth in your hands.

As you relish and even lock in this experience with your child, your mind might wander to the past (*I can't believe my baby is no longer chubby and round—look how long and slender he's become.*) or to the imagined future (*It won't be long before you don't need me to do this for you anymore*—with either a relieved *yay!* or a resigned *sigh*...). Gently continue to redirect your attention back to the little one in front of you here *now*, and allow yourself to bask in the warmth of the bath, your love, and your little blessing.

Reading

As I settle myself onto his bed in preparation for story time, my four-year-old chooses two books and then flops onto my lap, where he has perched comfortably for our ritual pre-nap and pre-bedtime reading since infancy. Considering this, I am suddenly amazed at the length of this little body resting on my lap. When did it happen? How is it possible that his feet stretch all the way down past my knees when I can easily recall the tiny bundle he was such a short time ago? He grows so fast that at times it seems like a time-lapse video happening before my very eyes. How do we interact with them so closely day after day but only register this growth in fits and spurts?

I think about my daughter as a little girl. Before she learned to read there were bedtimes, much like her speedy bath times, when I was so intent on completing the evening routine that I skipped whole paragraphs and pages just so I could tuck her in, be done with it, and get to some me-time. Inevitably, the time came when she said, "Huh? That makes no sense," after I unwittingly skipped over a crucial page, calling me out on my trickery as she began to recognize words on her own. Eventually we progressed from me reading solely to her, to her reading the simple books to me, to our taking turns reading aloud to each other.

> It's not only children who grow. Parents do too.
>
> *—Joyce Maynard*

Now, if I'm lucky, my daughter will join me on my bed at night as we sit side-by-side reading from our respective books. I look over at this lovely teenager, whose legs reach farther down the bed than mine, and am filled with disbelief that I might have wished that time away. I have compassion for that tired mom, I do. But I also am saddened by her need to rush through everything just to get to her own quiet time. It's my nature to want to check things off the list, but I have learned the value of slowing down and enjoying the ride more, even when I am tired and spent.

"Mom? Mom? Are you going to read?" My little guy's words wrench me out of my nostalgic reverie and straight back into the present moment. It's amazing how far and how quickly my mind can wander off the present moment into musing, planning, or worry. Yes, this is what our minds do—all the time. Whether while meditating formally or going about our day, we work with the wandering thoughts the same way—firmly and kindly return our attention to right now, forgive ourselves for wandering off yet again, take a deep breath, and begin afresh.

Of course, I sometimes still find my mind drifting off onto other plans as I read to my little guy (I have to say I am amazed at the mind's ability to think of completely other things while reading aloud) and have no recollection of what I just read to him.

But I do know from experience that this special reading time will end long before I am ready, so I breathe, bring myself back, and enter the world of Thomas the Tank Engine, *Star Wars*, and Superheroes once again.

The Reading Mindful Break: If it's time to read at bedtime and you are feeling especially tired and resistant, see if you can choose the shorter books and accept the sleepiness that will accompany the night's reading. On those nights when there is more time and energy to spare, allow a more leisurely pace and longer books. If you are like me and find the stories themselves less than captivating (monster trucks again?), use this time as a deliberate mindfulness practice session. Your mind will wander. You may encounter boredom, restlessness, or sleepiness. Notice it, accept it, take a deep breath, and redirect your attention to those words on the page connecting you to your child—that little body pressed up against yours—and the time that will one day be a memory you savor.

Recap the Day

"Let's talk about the day!" This has become a nightly bedtime routine in our house. Recounting the events of the day helps little ones integrate their experiences and make sense of events and memory. Because it postpones bedtime by another few moments, my little guy is happy to oblige.

My son still takes an afternoon nap (thank you, napping gods) and therefore often confuses nap time and nighttime sleeping. He may wake from a nap wondering if it's time to go to preschool or wake in the morning thinking it's dinnertime. Recapping the day in the evening helps put things into perspective for him and affords me the opportunity to lie in his bed next to him, our faces inches apart, and gaze into those deep brown eyes that melt me. It also reminds me once again how it's the smallest, most mundane moments that count just as much, if not more, than the big, carefully orchestrated ones. The bonding created through our nightly ritual of recapping the day settles us both in and seems to reassure him that all is well in his little world.

Our bedtime synopsis often begins with, "Today, you woke up early . . . as usual" (we both say in unison). We might talk about whom he saw, where he went, and how he spent his day in general.

It reinforces for us both that nothing momentous needs to transpire to have a wonderful, meaningful day. And on those days when something noteworthy occurred, it offers us a chance to savor the experience a bit more. The science of memory integration is what initiated the habit, but the feeling of enhanced connection between the two of us is why we continue to recap the day night after night.

The Recap the Day Mindful Break: Essentially, it matters little what actually occurred during the day. Whether the most exciting adventure or the most mundane of days, it's the recounting that counts in the shared experience.

Find a comfortable place to lie down and relax with your child, perhaps in her bed or snuggled up together in a comfy chair. Depending on her age, see if she can recall some noteworthy events from her day on her own. This often takes some practice and prompting from you. You can go into as much or as little detail as you'd like. Perhaps choose one or two experiences and probe a bit deeper with questions such as, "What was that like for you?" or "How do you think your friend felt when you invited her to play with you on the slide?" Take your cues from your child. If she prefers to keep it short and sweet, by all means do so, although if you've got a bedtime procrastinator on your hands you may need to draw the line at some point. Be curious, be interested, and just be there.

Partner Time

One of my all-time favorite TV shows, *Parenthood*, is a true-to-life series about four grown children, their parents, and their respective families. The patriarch, Zeek, is the veteran tough guy married to their artsy, tolerant mother for forty years. After some issues arise in their marriage, they attend couples therapy, where Zeek is advised to simply listen rather than attempt to fix. Instead of immediately jumping in with a solution, he is taught to first respond to his wife with the words, "I see you, I hear you."

Initially, he falls into his typical pattern, then catches himself, pauses, and repeats the given phrase. As their deeply ingrained communication pattern slowly changes, it's clear that something in his wife begins to break loose and shift as well. She is seen. She is heard. Whoa. Acted beautifully and played out with some humor, it's a poignant demonstration of what we all long for—to be seen and to be heard, especially by those who matter most to us.

Watching this story line unfold, my eyes welled up with tears. Touched to the core, I realized that I am often Zeek. And so is my husband. Amid the fullness of our lives, somewhere along the line we fell into an unhealthy habit of not seeing each other and only sometimes hearing each other. Not deliberately. Not out of lack of love or respect for each other, but because we allowed life to slowly creep in and take over.

> Show up and choose to be present.
> Pay attention to what has heart and meaning.
> Tell the truth without blame or judgment.
> Be open rather than attached to outcome.
>
> *—Angeles Arrien*

Is this a familiar scenario in your house? You have been out for the afternoon, return home, and walk into the house, happy to greet your family. As you come upon your kids, your face lights up in a big grin and you utter a heartfelt, "Hey! How are you?" as you grab them and hug them tightly. The dog comes running to you to be briefly petted, which you also bestow lovingly. Moving toward your partner, you offer a lukewarm, "Hey, how's it going?" and a quick peck on the lips before unpacking the groceries and falling into the rhythm of a bustling family.

Stop. Notice the difference. Reflect for a moment on how it unfolds in your household. If yours looks similar to this scenario, you are not alone. The incongruity of the basic human desire to be seen and daily reality with kids can be remarkable. Especially when the kids are small and take so much of our physical energy and time, at the end of a long day it can be difficult to make time for our partners.

There have been evenings when I could barely form a coherent sentence, let alone use the mental capacity for a deep, meaningful conversation with my husband. Conversely, there are the times when I am feeling chatty and energetic but he is exhausted from a stressful day. It's challenging to be in sync. I hear this sentiment repeated frequently when working with couples. It's easy to allow our partners to fall to the bottom of our list of priorities, but it's so important that we don't.

Remember what it felt like when you and your partner were first together, staring lovingly, all misty-eyed at each other? Bet you felt seen and heard then. Bet your partner did, too. It may not be possible to re-create the intensity of new love, but you can certainly move in that direction by offering your partner your full attention. You can see and hear him fully. The good news is that relationships can thrive with much less quality time than they did before kids joined your universe. But there must be some quality time, and we must be consistent if we want our relationships to grow and benefit.

The Partner Time Mindful Break: If you are like the majority of parents, there is not much kid-free together time going on so you must make the most of the time you have. Before anything else, I beg you to put away those electronics. Step away from the phone. If you are an electronics addict, it might be especially hard, but it becomes so much easier after a bit of practice. Initially, you may need to schedule this time to connect. Protect it. It's also healthy for the kids to see their parents prioritize, respect, and love each other through mindful communication.

You know what it feels like when someone is truly interested in what you have to say, when you have her full attention? Offer that to your partner. With so many distractions—kids, electronics, everyday responsibilities—competing for our attention, it's a true gift to tune into our beloveds for even just a few moments. Sit down. Face each other. Take a few deep breaths. As best you can, let go, just for these few moments, of all that still needs to be done. Settle in and be there as fully as you would with your child. Look into his eyes. See him, hear him. Over time, this simple practice can shift the entire feel of the relationship and bring you even closer.

Waiting Up

Waiting up for our children to come home at night is a rite of passage many parents would rather do without. Not only are we waiting up to hear the relieving click of the key turning in the lock, but also we're anticipating our children's relative state of happiness or discontent. We might even be waiting to appraise their sobriety.

While awaiting our precious progeny's return, several imagined scenarios might play out in our concerned mommy minds. Perhaps we envision them having a wonderful time as we hypothesize about what they are doing and with whom they are talking. More often than not, though, our busy minds veer toward the negative, the anxious, and occasionally the horrific thoughts we wouldn't dare speak out loud. While we are waiting we might unwittingly visualize all sorts of outlandish (or realistic) movies in our restless minds. As we have now recognized through mindfulness, our thoughts can be persistent and sneaky, taking us on wild rides we would much rather forgo.

But can you blame our busy mommy minds? After all, we're not sure what we're going to encounter when our teenagers walk

> In the end, just three things matter: How well we have lived. How well we have loved. How well we have learned to let go.
>
> *—Jack Kornfield*

through that door. Depending on your child, his social and behavioral history, his age as well as numerous other variables (including our own inherent level of anxiety and worry) determine what we imagine, fear, and hope for. Will he be beaming ear-to-ear with tales of a fantastic night? Will he walk in and offer a lukewarm hug before retreating to his room with nary a comment? Will she burst into your bedroom, tears spilling from her eyes as she recounts a deep hurt inflicted by a trusted friend? Will she respect curfew? Will you need to look into her eyes, assessing the possible influence of substances? It's the unpredictability of the situation that can be the most challenging.

When our children return home safe and sound, we can breathe a sigh of relief. However, there may still be the quandary of dealing with an unpleasant situation if it has arisen. Whether facing obvious substance use, an emotionally painful night, or a broken curfew, we moms must keep ourselves in check before we can attend to our children's needs, whatever they may require in the moment. Because we hurt when they hurt and we are only as happy as our least happy child, keeping ourselves calm needs to be the first order of business. Only then can we mindfully face the situation at hand.

The Waiting Up Mindful Break: While you're waiting, take a moment to pause and notice the flavor of your thoughts. Are they riddled with anxiety and worry? Are you what-iffing repeatedly? Or are you imagining your child engaged in a positive, pleasing evening? Is your mind playing out a warm, lighthearted exchange or a heated one upon her return home?

First notice and name the thoughts you're experiencing and then redirect and distract if necessary. Offer yourself compassion for this universal parenting challenge and know that you are not alone. If your thoughts are repeatedly replaying worries, after you have noticed and acknowledged them it may be time to engage in some healthy distraction. But choose your distraction wisely, allowing it to include some self-care. This may be a perfect time to meditate, spend time with your partner, or read a magazine.

When your child does return home, first breathe and relax your body. Offer a hug. Be there fully to reconnect and listen mindfully, which may mean applying imaginary duct tape to your mouth. Perhaps silently offer gratitude for his safe return, the ultimate in parental relief. Whether pleasant or daunting, you are now ready to tackle whatever comes next.

Prepping for Tomorrow

If you or any of your children have a morning schedule requiring you to be up, ready, and out of the house at a relatively early time, I strongly encourage you to experiment with this mindful break. Spending a few moments each evening preparing as much as possible for the following day, especially on weekdays, can create a much more fluid, harmonious start to your morning. Ultimately, I find that the less brain power I need to expend in the morning before caffeine, the better—for all of us in my household. It takes ten minutes to prep in the evening, but it pays off in dividends the next morning. Those ten extra minutes on an early weekday morning are invaluable for both basic logistics and my sanity.

In our house, the evening prep consists of ensuring the kitchen is cleaned up following dinner, because what I certainly do not want to face at 5 AM is a sink full of unwashed dishes. I fill and set my beloved coffeemaker for its ungodly early brewing time, place my small-bowl–size mug next to it in quiet anticipation, set the table with silverware and vitamins for the morning, assemble my lunch (most often leftovers packed while cleaning up dinner), gather my little guy's backpack if needed, and charge electronic devices.

I taught my daughter to prep for the next day as well. I'm quite sure we both began the habit when she transitioned to middle school because she needed to catch the school bus at a very early hour. Each evening she packs her lunch, gym bag, and book bag. This system necessitated first nightly, then sporadic reminders for a few months before it became an ingrained habit she now undertakes without any prompting. Children as young as preschool age can learn how to create this mindful break with some continued encouragement and coaching.

On those mornings when I have not prepped the evening before, the pace feels rushed and my thoughts feel scattered; there simply is more to be done in a limited amount of time. For me, not prepping feels similar to not meditating that morning. I do manage to get it all done, but I am much less on my game and certainly much less at ease, which, we know, trickles down to the family. On those mornings when I have not prepared, I start the day feeling increased stress, often leaving me exhausted before my day at work even begins. Prepping the night before offers us all an opportunity to breathe and begin the day with a sense of ease. This is not only a gift to myself, but to my children as well—not only for each morning filled with more ease, but for their formation of healthy habits over the long haul.

The Prepping for Tomorrow Mindful Break: If you are just forming this mindful break as a new habit, mentally run through your morning as it now plays out. Note as many tasks as possible that can be completed the night before. It may be helpful initially to jot down a quick list to refer to until this new mindful break becomes ingrained. Before you begin prepping, pause and take a deep breath in and out. Bring your full attention to each part of the routine. When your mind wanders, even to just the next task at hand, gently redirect your awareness to that in which you are engaged. You may want to bring a sense of gratitude for the abundance of food to nourish, vitamins to support health, and coffee to survive.

Assess which tasks your children can prepare ahead of time as well and teach them their respective responsibilities. This will take time and repeated, and I do mean repeated, reminders from you. Be patient. On those mornings when their prep has been completed the night prior, reinforce with them how much more smoothly the morning runs. Let them learn and appreciate first-hand the value of this mindful break.

Progressive Muscle Relaxation

Do you ever have trouble shutting down your mind when bedtime rolls around? Do you ever lie down at the end of the evening, bone-tired from a full day, yet find yourself unable to fall asleep due to the busyness of your mind? This rarely happens to me. In fact, placing my body in a horizontal position at any point during the day is an invitation for sleep to overtake me almost instantly.

Before you fantasize about throwing this book at my head due to my seemingly awesome ability to sleep, hold on just a second. Dozing off at bedtime is not my challenge, but being roused in the middle of the night most certainly is. Whether I am awakened by a child needing water to soothe a cough or to be tucked back in after a bad dream, I can almost guarantee I will remain awake for the next hour or two, like it or not. Regardless of how long I spent soothing or tucking, my mind is now wide awake and ready to go.

I have learned (mostly) not to fight it. When I start imagining how tired I will be in the morning, I remind myself that I can lie there, close my eyes, and some rest will still occur. Sometimes I practice a Progressive Muscle Relaxation Mindful Break to calm my body, especially if I'm feeling physically restless. I may follow it with some awareness of breath meditation or a body scan (pages 42–43) while lying in bed. Often this will allow my mind to settle more easily and sleep to arrive a bit sooner.

So whether your sleep challenge is falling asleep, getting back to sleep, or none of the above (lucky you), this practice is about creating the conditions for a good night's sleep as best you can, then surrendering to however it plays out that evening. Sleep, for better or worse, cannot be forced but can be gently encouraged with some progressive muscle relaxation.

The Progressive Muscle Relaxation Mindful Break: Regardless of your level of difficulty with sleep, progressive muscle relaxation can aid in the transition from daily movement to the stillness of sleep and is done by squeezing the muscles in each body part, in turn, for five seconds, then releasing with an exhale. Beginning with the feet, tense the muscles in each foot as tightly as possible, and after five seconds, release and breathe out. Next, tighten the calf muscles for five seconds and then let go. Slowly move up the body, part by part, until you have made your way to the face and head. After all the individual body parts have been attended to, squeeze all the muscles in the entire body at once and then release, allowing the body to become soft, relaxed, and completely supported by the bed.

I wish I could promise you immediate entry into dreamland, but unfortunately there are no sleep guarantees. Progressive muscle relaxation does help release some restlessness and increases overall body awareness. If you are alert enough to practice it, you are already a captive audience and might as well put that wakeful time to some good self-care use. Wishing you plenty of sweet dreams. . . .

2 AM Wake-Up Calls

Ah, sleep. I have a love-hate relationship with you. I love the rest, the release, the recharging. I hate that I never seem to get enough of you. "Hate is a strong word," I tell my kids. But in this case, it most certainly applies. Oh, sleep. There are so many varying degrees of you: plain sleepy, brain-fogged, exhausted, bone-tired to I-just-want-to-lie-down-and-cry tired. I've experienced you all, and I don't think I've had enough of you since I became a mom fourteen years ago.

After my little guy was born, I grew to understand why the military uses sleep deprivation as an effective form of torture. I would've told them anything they wanted to know and then some. Sleep, you became like an obsession, an addiction, something I craved desperately, clung to, wished for, imagining a day when you'd be completely under my control. When will you not be interrupted? Oh, sleep, I do miss you. When will I get enough of you? When the little guy goes off to college? Only another fourteen years to go. *Sigh*. This is what my thoughts sound like when I am sleep deprived, except a lot less lucid. Yes, my wearied mind can indeed become a scary place.

When my toddler calls out in the middle of the night, I pry my eyes open, look over at my husband who remains blissfully asleep, and grumble, "Really? Not. My. Turn." When I am tired, my reserves are down, and patience is in short supply, I often find myself silently keeping score with my husband. *I got up last time. I have more on my plate right now. How can you possibly sleep through this?* We all know how helpful this score-keeping game is—not at all. In reality, my husband is a wonderful husband and father, a willing co-parent not at all married to stereotypical gender roles. Any sense of objectivity goes right out the window, however, when I am in this most unhelpful state of mind.

When I find myself pulled into this pessimistic place, the most beneficial thing I have learned to do is to begin a thought with *I get to* instead of *I have to*. Rather than *I have to* get up at 2 AM, *I get to* cuddle the little guy for a few minutes, savoring the lingering scent of baby shampoo on his head of soft, curly hair. It doesn't help every time, but it works more often than not.

Regardless of what is occurring in our lives, we have a choice to live in an *I get to* mindset or one of *I have to*. It's a gentle practice, not to be forced and not meant to induce guilt when *I have to* remains resolute. It's not artificial and, as a therapist, I would never recommend we ignore or deny important emotions or realizations that may need to be addressed. But in that moment of resistance, am I willing to nudge myself in the direction of *I get to*, thereby subtly shifting my attitude and naturally reconnecting with gratitude—gratitude for the countless blessings in my life—my children, my husband, our health? I may never enjoy being awakened at 2 AM, but with a mindful *I get to*, my attitude may soften into one of reconnecting to the privilege of being Mom to this beautiful (any time of the day or night) little boy.

The 2 AM Wake-Up Calls Mindful Break: When you find that your perception has veered toward the negative, experiment with beginning a thought with *I get to* rather than *I have to*. It's vital that this not be forced but is rather a gentle encouragement in the shift of your approach. It is, paradoxically, most challenging to remember and to put into practice when we most need it.

Notice when the mental scorecard shows up. As best you can, let go of comparing and bring yourself back to the present moment, grounding yourself in the inhale and exhale of the breath. *I get to*. This choice of wording is often enough to remind us of the fleeting privilege of motherhood, allowing us to more easily accept and appreciate all that accompanies it—scary, bad neighborhoods notwithstanding.

MINDFULOG

Use this space to record your daily 5-Minute Meditations and mindful breaks. See page 15 for more details on how to make the most of the Mindfulog. For blank copies, visit shondamoralis.net.

MINDFUL PRACTICE	MONDAY	TUESDAY	WEDNESDAY
5-MINUTE MEDITATION			
MINDFUL BREAK			
MINDFUL BREAK			
MINDFUL BREAK			

THURSDAY	FRIDAY	SATURDAY	SUNDAY

BIBLIOGRAPHY

Alcorn, Katrina. "Do You Have a Hospital Fantasy?" huffingtonpost.com, August 24, 2011.

———. *Maxed Out: American Moms on the Brink*. Berkeley: Seal Press, 2013.

Bolte Taylor, Jill. *My Stroke of Insight: A Brain Scientist's Personal Journey*. New York: Viking, 2008.

Brach, Tara. "Guided Meditations." tarabrach.com/guided-meditations.

Brown, Brené. *Daring Greatly: How the Courage to Be Vulnerable Transforms the Way We Live, Love, Parent, and Lead*. New York: Gotham, 2012.

Carter, Christine. *Raising Happiness: 10 Simple Steps for More Joyful Kids and Happier Parents*. New York: Ballantine, 2010.

Cuddy, Amy. *Presence: Bringing Your Boldest Self to Your Biggest Challenges*. New York: Little, Brown and Company, 2015.

———. "Your Body Language Shapes Who You Are," ted.com.

Davidson, Richard J., Jon Kabat-Zinn, Jessica Schumacher, Melissa Rosenkranz, Daniel Muller, Saki F. Santorelli, Ferris Urbanowski, Anne Harrington, Katherine Bonus, and John F. Sheridan. "Alterations in Brain and Immune Function Produced by Mindfulness Meditation." *Psychosomatic Medicine* 65, no. 4 (2003): 564–70.

——— and Sharon Begley. *The Emotional Life of Your Brain*. New York: Hudson Street Press, 2012.

Dell'Antonia, KJ. *The New York Times Motherlode* blog. "Hey, Whiny, Modern Parents, Tell Us What You Love About the Gig." parenting.blogs.nytimes.com, April 28, 2014.

Fredrickson, B. L., M. A. Cohn, K. A. Coffey, J. Pek, and S. M. Finkel, "Open Hearts Build Lives: Positive Emotions, Induced Through Loving-Kindness Meditation, Build Consequential Personal Resources." *Journal of Personality and Social Psychology* 95, no. 5 (2008): 1045.

Goldstein, Elisha David. "Sacred Moments: Implications on Well-Being and Stress." Special Issue on Spirituality and Psychotherapy, *Journal of Clinical Psychology* 63, no. 10 (October 2007): 1001–19.

Hölzel, Britta K., S. Lazar, T. Gard, Z. Schuman-Olivier, D. R. Vago, and U. Ott. 2011. "How Does Mindfulness Meditation Work? Proposing Mechanisms of Action from a Conceptual and Neural Perspective." *Perspectives on Psychological Science* 6, no 6: 537–59.

Kabat-Zinn, Myla, and Jon Kabat-Zinn. *Everyday Blessings: The Inner Work of Mindful Parenting.* New York: Hyperion, 1997.

Kabat-Zinn, Jon. "Heartfulness." Omega Institute for Holistic Studies. youtube.com.

Lahey, Jessica. *The Gift of Failure: How the Best Parents Learn to Let Go So Their Children Can Succeed.* New York: HarperCollins, 2015.

Lerner, Harriet. *The Mother Dance: How Children Change Your Life.* New York: HarperCollins, 2009.

Morrish, Ronald. *Secrets of Discipline: For Parents and Teachers.* Foothill, Ontario, Canada: Woodstream Publishing, 1997.

Moyer, Christopher A., Michael PW Donnelly, Jane C. Anderson, Kally C. Valek, Sarah J. Huckaby, Derek A. Wiederholt, Rachel

L. Doty, Aaron S. Rehlinger, and Brianna L. Rice. "Frontal Electroencephalographic Asymmetry Associated with Positive Emotion Is Produced by Very Brief Meditation Training." *Psychological Science* 22, no. 10 (2011): 1277–79.

Payne, Kim John, with Lisa M. Ross. *Simplicity Parenting: Using the Extraordinary Power of Less to Raise Calmer, Happier, and More Secure Kids*. New York: Ballantine, 2009.

Race, Kristen. *Mindful Parenting: Simple and Powerful Solutions for Raising Creative, Engaged, Happy Kids in Today's Hectic World*. New York: St. Martin's Press, 2013.

Rhimes, Shonda. *Year of Yes: How to Dance It Out, Stand in the Sun and Be Your Own Person*. New York: Simon and Schuster, 2015.

Senior, Jennifer. "For Parents, Happiness Is a Very High Bar." ted .com.

Shapiro, Shauna, and Chris White. *Mindful Discipline: A Loving Approach to Setting Limits and Raising an Emotionally Intelligent Child*. Oakland: New Harbinger, 2014.

Siegel, Daniel J. *Mindsight: The New Science of Personal Transformation*. New York: Bantam Books, 2010.

Willey, Kira. Official Web site. kirawilley.com.

ACKNOWLEDGMENTS

So much gratitude, so little time. Thanks to Erik for your support, sense of humor, and keeping us well fed and cared for while I stole off to write each week. To Mom and Dad, I could not have done it without your help. Words cannot express how blessed I am to be your daughter. To Ani and Ben, thanks for your patience, understanding, and love. You are my truest joys and inspiration. Thanks to my wonderful agent, Claire Gerus. I so appreciate your guidance. I was lucky enough to score two wonderful editors, Jennifer Boudinot and Sue Fisher. To my publisher Matthew Lore, Jennifer Hergenroeder, Batya Rosenblum, Sarah Smith, and everyone at The Experiment, thanks for your belief in me and your dedication to this project. Together we have created something of which I am immensely proud.

To Roger Yepsen, I owe you a debt of gratitude for your time and wisdom, and to Ali Nass-Yepsen for being a supportive mindful friend and mentor. To Barbara Berger for cheering me on through the whole process. To Renell Carpenter for your astute early edits, and to Kira Willey for your encouragement and insights. Thanks to all the Monthly Tea and Mindfulness Mamas (especially Amy Dangler and Maria Schaller) whose wisdom, laughter, and creativity never cease to amaze me. To Signe

Whitson, Carla Naumburg, and Joyce Hinnefeld for encouraging a novice author in conversations.

To Hunter Clarke-Fields for offering the opportunity to share my message. To singer-songwriter Susan Werner for generously sharing your gift. To Joanne Cohen-Katz, Susan Wiley, and the Lehigh Valley Health Network Center for Mindfulness, who taught me much of what I know about mindfulness. To my Panera group: Kathleen Gavin, Melanie Himmelberger, and Dina Lomas, for your ongoing support. To everyone at Twin Ponds Integrative Health Center—thanks for a warm, welcoming place to work and write. Thanks to my early readers and neighbors: Karen Walczer, Nancy Wood, Beth Smith, Trish Smith, and Rosemarie Lister. To Dr. Allie Gaines for her early insights, especially breast-feeding meditation. Thanks to my friends Nicole Wade, Amy Godshall, Kim Hayes, my brother, Brian Bear, and sister-in-law, Cynthia Visser, for following me on this journey. And thanks, especially, to all of you moms out there who have shared your stories with me over the years. You inspire me.

NOTES

NOTES

NOTES

NOTES

NOTES

ABOUT THE AUTHOR

SHONDA MORALIS, MSW, LCSW, is a psychotherapist in private practice specializing in stress-related disorders and mindfulness-based therapy. She writes the *Psychology Today* blog *Breathe, Mama, Breathe* and her own blog, *Mindfultalk,* at shondamoralis.net. Moralis has developed and taught mindfulness courses and workshops for children, parents, teachers, and students. She lives with her husband and two children in the Lehigh Valley, Pennsylvania.